This Side of Tragedy

Psychotherapy as Theater

By Sheldon Kopp

Science and Behavior Books, Inc.
701 Welch Road
Palo Alto, California, 94306

Library of Congress Catalog Card Number: 75-45904
ISBN Number: 8314-0050-1

To Lora Price
Who is a continuing source of delight
in my life. She brings her wonderful
sense of theater to both the starring
roles of loving friend and of
talented psychotherapist.

TABLE OF CONTENTS

Part I
THE THEATER OF THERAPY

Part II
THE PLAY OPENS

Part III
TRAGEDY AND BEYOND

Part I
The Theater of Therapy

Chapter I
Miscasting

Life is sometimes painful, often unfair, perhaps always absurd, but tragic, it is *not*. We use the words "tragic" and "tragedy" so loosely and so often, that they have come to *seem* to describe accurately what appear to be *universal* human experiences of undeserved calamity. Any disturbing spectacle of unwarranted suffering gets to be called "tragic." Someone dies young; an adult is crippled while trying to rescue a trapped child; "innocent" civilians are killed or maimed by war. Newspaper headlines and television commentators tell us it is a *tragedy*. We shake our heads, feel pity for the undeserving victims, fear for ourselves and our loved ones, and helplessness before the inevitability of cruel Fate.

The tragic immersion of the characters in certain classical dramas make for a moving theater experience just because their suffering evokes an empathic note in each member of the audience. Not that we too each live heroically tragic lives, but rather because we each have our moments. Everyone has gone through brief episodes of daemonic possession, overpowering instances which allow us to identify with the exaggerated dramatization of character of the tragic hero. Who has not lost his temper, fallen in love, been caught up in over-riding enthusiasms, ego-tripped, or even freaked out?

For most of us such willful actions, dramatic bits, and exaggerated parts are highlights rather than life roles. The results may be briefly exciting, scary, or messy. Rarely are they irreversibly catastrophic.

Each of us gets in over his head from time to time, stubbornly playing out a momentarily bigger-than-life fantasy. Sometimes these episodic daemonic states of possession may take the form of collective madness. Yielding to foolishly inflated social demands can over-ride the good sense of a whole group of people, submerging personal expression to some "higher" purpose. For some of us, the taking on of miscast roles may involve the more chronic, life-time acting out of a neurotic personal "tragedy."

Life is so damned complicated. There doesn't seem to be any way for any of us to get through a day without spending some part of it playing out temporary roles. We perform rehearsed social, or even personal actions which do *not* engage or reveal very much of who we really are. Surely the actor is more than any part he happens to be playing at the moment. Sometimes we confuse the actor with the part, or the Self with the mask. We then risk losing our way in a House of Mirrors as we mistake illusion for reality.

Too often, as children, we are encouraged to try to be something other than ourselves. It is demanded that we assume a character not our own, live out a life-story written by another. The plot line is given. Improvisations are unacceptable, and the direction is an oppressive form of close-quarter tyranny. Neurosis is in part the result of being miscast into a scenario plotted out in accord with somebody else's unfulfilled dreams and unfaced anxieties.

As a result of the personal unhappiness that comes of such miscasting, unconvincing performers such as these sometimes appear in that theatrical setting known as psychotherapy. They bill themselves as tragic figures and ostensibly they come to hire the therapist to rewrite their script, or at best to serve as an acting coach. But in the psychotherapeutic montage of illusion and reality, patient and therapist take turns as performers, audience, director, and playwright, during their tumultuous limited engagement.[1]

In my own family, the miscasting was confoundingly comprehensive. The part of Mother was played by my Dad, while Mom starred as Father. They always played each other's role, and so, my mother was my father, and my father was my mother. It's been just that confused and confusing from the opening curtain.

You will find that some of my complaints are not unlike Portnoy's.[2] Many neurotic scripts sound Jewish. The Children of Israel are historically committed to a religiously heroic tragic vision of themselves and their sufferings. They suffer in the name of God. Their Covenant/contract with the Lord calls for their having to endure pain and unhappiness for His namesake. All of this is a tribute to His greatness, but more to the point, it is a way of defining their own special place in history.

The tragic flaw of the Jew is his great devotion. His history of persecution and catastrophe demonstrates that *his* devotion is better than that of ordinary men. In this lies the absurd truth that "Jews are just like everyone else, only more so." Not that they are more human (as some would claim) but that they are more stylized, more caricatured, more foolishly heroic.

Being one of these Chosen People instructs me in the absurdity of the tragic heroic pose. But as a Jew, I may also learn to be saved by the comic element in my life, though it be by gallows humor. Only by discovering the absurdity of my needless suffering and by learning not to take myself too seriously may I save myself from a life-long role of the tragic hero. Life is too important to be taken seriously.

Let us return to the opening scenes of my own tragic miscasting. The time is the beginning of the Great Depression. The place, a small apartment in the Bronx, U.S.A. The physical appearances and costumes of the family members are appropriate to their stations in life.

But look more closely. You will see that their lines, their acting, and their character development set up a bewildering array of episodes of mistaken identity. My mother, a dark-haired Rose, had the buxom bosom and full hips which her original part demanded. My father in contrast was tall, slim, and wiry, a bit dapper, but recognizable as a product of the streets of Hell's Kitchen in which he grew up. Add to that my own appearance as a cuddly baby and an appealing toddler, not looking unlike other babies and toddlers elsewhere, and you have a cast whose pictures would have made adequate publicity stills. You simply cannot tell from the family photo album that I was already the villain.

From the opening lines, it was clear that we were all miscast. My mother turned out to be a domineering, ambitious, aggressive Jewish lady who hated to cook. She boasted being "a better businessman than your father ever was." My father on the other hand was passive and soft spoken, tender when he was present. Seeming only to want peace and quiet, he met my mother's daily onslaughts with the plaintive plea: "But, Rosie, Rosie, I love you."

I am not making a case for what a baby should be or what the male and female parental roles should be. But growing up in the Thirties and Forties, I found such profound deviations from the type-casting of that period totally bewildering. As if all of that was not confusion enough, we had a canary named "Tarzan."

I myself was cast a conception as the villain of the piece. It was as though my folks could/have, would/have lived the happy lives which good children deserved, if only *I had not played the bad parent.* They were fine and life went well until I entered from the wings. From the start I made mother nervous, gave her pain, and endangered her very life. I was billed as a sort of *foetus ex machina.*

The pregnancy was awful, the labor long, and the delivery ill-timed. At about one a.m. on the morning of March 29, 1929, at the (of course) Royal Hospital in the Bronx, my mother complained about how much trouble I was already. She assured my father that I would keep her in pain all night by not making my debut till dawn. He was instructed to go home and get a good night's sleep. On cue, he made the mistake of following her instructions. I appeared on stage at 3 a.m., plunging him into a mess for which he would be berated for years afterward.

Neither my father nor I were ever allowed to forget our poor performances. when I did appear, the hospital staff summoned him from home. Arriving at the hospital and learning that I was a boy, he knew he was in for even more trouble. He had promised my mother I would be a girl. At first, he avoided mother's touchiness about such matters and delayed the bad scene which would follow. When he first spoke to her as she emerged from the protective anaesthetic, he *pretended* to her that I was the daughter she had ordered.

The nurse insisted on telling her that I was a boy. She brought me in to show me to the disappointed couple, and they made the necessary revisions in my casting. Once I was old enough to understand, my mother told me the story again and again. She recounted how when they first saw me all that was visible were my "long skinny fingers sticking out from under the *blue* blanket." "I knew right away," she would go on (and on), "that with such fingers you were destined to be a concert pianist . . . , or a strangler."

My father, for his part, delayed telling his tale. It was twenty-five years later when he first saw *my* own first-born son whom I offered to let him hold. He declined, "I can't. I never held you for the first six months. I was afraid I'd drop you." All I could reply was, "You dirty son-of-a-bitch."

As a daughter, I was to have been named Judith. As a son, I was named for a recent dead relative (in the traditional Jewish manner). My Jewish name is Shimin, named for my great Aunt Sarah. Fool with that one for a while!

And so from my opening scene I was miscast as the unredeemed sinner, the heavy of the plot whose actions (and mere presence) posed endless problems for the starring parents. Because of their commitments to show what good parents they were no matter how bad a child I was, we were caught up in a contemporary tragedy. My mother's summary one-liner (delivered when I was an early adolescent) was, "I love you, but I don't like you." I of course understood the intention of this line. She was telling me that I was to be burdened by the loyalty of a good mother to a bad child. I in turn had the hopeless responsibility of finding out how to be good so that my parents could be happy once more (as they had purportedly been before my entrance).

For a while I believed that I was such a bad boy that it was no wonder to me that I was punished so often. Not by my father. He rarely openly showed any anger toward me. I can only remember his hitting me two or three times in my life, and then only because I had upset my mother. For many years he took me on trips, mostly to museums, and taught me many things.

His own father had been a strange Hungarian alcoholic, a man who was well-educated, spoke many languages, and never worked. Instead he turned my Dad's tenement apartment to an unsuccessful salon, one in which he held forth on matters intellectual to anyone in the neighborhood who would listen. His chronic complaint was that he was surrounded by ignorance.

My father wanted to learn from his own father. My

grandfather turned him away saying he was a stupid boy who would never be wise. How my father wanted to be wise. He loved school but had to quit in the sixth grade to get a regular job. Up to that point his place in the family's subsistence economy was fulfilled by going down to the docks and throwing stones at the men who worked on the passing coal barges. They would try to pelt my father with coal which he would collect in a sack and take home to warm the family's railroad flat.

My father educated himself, and swore that he would treat me the way his father should have treated him. As a small child my very favorite bed-time story was The Death of Socrates. He taught me much, but he sold me out to my mother. The only form of criticism I received from him was, "Stop upsetting your mother." By the time I was ten, he had yielded to her pressures for him to stop being a failure, and earn some more money. This was accomplished by his trying to be a better husband and father by working out-of-town (on the road) six months out of the year. He left me home to deal with that crazy woman all by myself.

My mother pushed me to be strong from as early a time as I can remember. She gave me power, confidence, recklessness, and more responsibility and guilt than a kid can manage. She had grown up in a family in which her own mother had had eleven children and four miscarriages, then her father ran off with another woman. Up to that point he had been "a poor tailor," seeingly acceeding to my grandmother's wishes. Now they knew that he had really been no good from the start. If only my grandmother had known in time, she could have prevented this disaster.

It would be different with me. If it was up to my mother I would turn out to be reliable, responsible, sensitive, and considerate, even if she had to beat it into me. She hurt me often when I was a kid. She pinched me (slowly), hit me with wooden hangers and metal spatulas. She was deadly with a high-heeled shoe from across the room. In a way it was a kindness. This cruelty was so open. Even *I* knew that it was more than I deserved.

By the time I was twelve (as soon as I was big enough), I grabbed her by the arms during one of these beatings. I held her wrists tight beside her so that she couldn't go on hitting me. I looked her in the eye and said: "I'm never going to let you hit me again."

At first I thought I'd said it so dramatically that it was no wonder that she was afraid to try anything like that again. Years later I realized that she was secretly pleased, as she complained to her sister about what I had done, complained in the winking way people do when they are boasting about something they're not supposed to be proud of.

This episode ended the beatings, but it did not end the miscasting. I seemed to have always known, and I continued to know that:

> *If not for me surely my good parents would have been*
> *happy. There seemed to be nothing that I could do or say*
> *which did not hurt them. I was desperate to learn to be*
> *like all the other children. I watched them and tried to do*
> *what they did, so that I too might learn to please. Seeing*
> *this, my parents would say, "See how hard he tries to be*
> *good, that bad boy." By the time I reached adolescence*
> *I gave up. It seemed that the only thing I really knew*
> *to do was to be bad. And so, with a vengeance, I got to be*
> *really good at being bad. I gave up passively finding my-*
> *self in trouble, and began actively to pursue the evil urge.*[3]

For many years I could not see the theatrical aspects of this painful family configuration. It was mystifying to me. I could get my parents so upset, hurt them so deeply, merely by using "a disrespectful tone of voice." Yet they made so little of any real danger into which I might put myself. I was fully grown before I realized that the issue was *not* whether I was doing anything truly dangerous or destructive. It was all a matter of not getting them upset by threatening to expose the near fatal theater-games in which we were engaged.

Perhaps I should have known from the nick-name they chose for me, my parents' only consistent term of affection in addressing me. They called me, *"Nisht Guteh."* It means "No Good One."

They said it in a way which always let me know when I was playing my part in a script I had never read.

Yet when I was beginning to do illegal, potentially dangerous things, they tended to play down any reason for concern. At fifteen, I was into dope and semi-delinquency. I hung out in physically dangerous settings where violence was frequent, where switch-blades and guns were common props. I tried to rescue myself, calling my parents' attention to the dangers, as if to say, "Look, Ma, I'm getting into trouble."

I would approach them about some dangerous setting I'd been in. At sixteen I'd found myself holding a junkie's arm strap, so that his mutilated vein would be made available for another fix. I'd come on deviously to my folks, saying something like, "Look I didn't want you to be upset because you heard it from someone else" (translation: "I'm telling you because otherwise I'm afraid you would never find out."). "I've been hanging around with dope fiends." "That's all right," they'd reassure me. "You're a smart boy. You'll never do that again."

Physical danger did not seem to be the issue. In retrospect it seems that what being "bad" referred to was expressing my feelings. I was not to be obviously beyond parental control. I was not to put my own needs ahead of theirs.

Even as an infant I was restrained at first by being wrapped in swaddling by a Russian peasant grandmother (to whom my mother sometimes offered me up as a ritual sacrifice). Later on I was told that whenever I was unwrapped even briefly from time to time, I immediately began to flail about. Someone would quickly insist that I be restrained once more because I was getting "too excited."

This refrain was repeated often as I grew older. I was playing too long. That was no good for me. I "fooled around" too long in the ocean surf which I so loved. It was time to get out. Not that I was cold or tired or in danger. It was time to get out because my mother said, "Too much is no good."

And what's more, I must come out willingly and without expressing any feelings that might question my mother's having my best interests at heart. It was the same as those times when I'd come home from school, eager to get out to the streets to play with the other kids. First, I would have to go to the store to buy something my mother had neglected to pick up. Refusal was out of the question. I was punished for even complaining. I was made to feel terribly unworthy if any gesture or postural attitude revealed my discontent. Her injunction was, "Don't throw yourself."

Years later with my own kids, we formulated a family rule to guard against such cruel restrictions. In line with what we had learned from Orwell's description of psychological tyranny in *Nineteen Eighty-Four*,[4] we rule out all "face-crimes."

In my early twenties, I heard the echo of my parents' injunctions against disrespect for authority. I was a man, married, about to be a father, a graduate student, and a self-supporting working psychologist being drafted into the Army during the Korean War. After breaking their promise to "Shoot me in the leg" themselves before they'd let me be a soldier, my parents' parting advice to me was "Don't be fresh to the officers!"

I was always "fresh." I could manage this simply by any intonation which revealed that there was a person-of-my-own somewhere down inside me. But to be sure, we developed this interplay into memorable vignettes which could then be recounted in the future as painful reminders of the proof that I was bad, or perhaps simply as running gags.

One such symbolic incident involved my using the expletive, "Hell" as a teenager in an argument with my mother. She was terribly shocked, though she herself frequently used terms like "shit" and "damn" in two or three languages. Her response was to instruct me: "First, a boy says 'Hell' to a Mother; then soon a boy will tell a Mother 'Go to 'Hell.'" I complied by delivering the specified line within two weeks. I'm a quick study.

Expression of my anger toward my family was thus to be restricted to modes which could be clearly labelled to keep me in character as a bad boy. But there were other sorts of assertion which I was encouraged to prepare for in the future in the world beyond the family. My parents indulged me in many material ways. They provided clothes, toys, money, entertainment and the like. My mother would say: "I want you to taste all the good things in the world, so that someday when you grow up you'll know what's good. And then you won't let anything stand in your way. You won't be weak like your father. You'll take what you want."

This aspect of my future role was assured by making me feel terribly guilty about whatever was given to me. When I asked for money as a kid, I was always given some. As the pennies were placed in my outstretched hand, I would be told, "Here, take it, whatever you want, you can have. Only remember, it's our heart's blood. Your father slaved for this money and I, God knows, went without. But for you, who else do we live for? Take it and enjoy!"

By the age of eleven, I was working. It was easier than being subjected to their generosity. I worked after school, weekends, and summers for many years, years when I should have been out playing.

Expression of my aggressiveness was to be directed toward the world beyond the family. How I was to experience my anxieties was to be dictated by this script as well. Some things were to be feared, non-Jewish things such as strange food. "You never know what *dreck* (shit) the *Goyim* (Gentiles) put in there." (Chow Mein and Pizza were somehow exceptions.)

Almost anything offered by someone outside the family (or the culture) must be approached with dread, since it was likely to be contaminated. "You never know where they had their hands last." And besides, "Family is everything. When no one else can be counted on, only Family will take care of you." "But Mom," I would protest, "What about your brother, Bill?" I knew she hated her oldest brother. He was a business rival of my father and my other uncles. He had tried to have them imprisoned for fraud more than once. Unphased, my mother would explain, "My brother Bill is *not* Family."

Anything that made her anxious was supposed to make me anxious as well. It was very confusion for a while. The script called for me to react in some ways which at first did not seem to fit the part. For example, I was told to say out of strange neighborhoods, especially back alleys. There lurked dangerous men, I was told, even when I was too young to quite understand what she meant. I must remember, she insisted, "They don't just like to get girls and do terrible things to them. They like fat little boys too." My subliminal understanding of this warning was surely reinforced by mother's traditional way of treating any sign of ill health I might show. Every time I turned around, it seemed, she would give me an enema.

Anxieties which did not fit the script simply were written out. There might be something scary my mother wanted me to do. If I made the mistake of complaining that I was afraid, she could clarify things immediately by *explaining*, "No, you're not. You're *not* afraid." That's funny. I had thought I was afraid. Gradually, I learned not to have any *rational* fears. I learned that I could do anything that my mother set her mind to. Surely I could become the success my father was not.

Whatever training I needed was provided. I began getting assignments when I was quite young. At about age eight, I lost a glove, one of a new pair. I was sent on a round of knocking at each door in our apartment complex. There were probably only thirty, but it seemed like a hundred at the time. I was to tell each neighbor that my parents had bought me a lovely, expensive pair of gloves. I carelessly had lost one. It was my responsibility to find out if anyone in the building had found the misplaced glove.

By the time I was ten or eleven, I had graduated to more commercial assignments. I remember being sent down to the local butcher shop with a package of meat which she had purchased earlier that day. The shop was always filled with local Jewish lady customers crowding impatiently around the display counters. Behind the counters were great powerful, foreign-sounding butcher-men dressed in bloody aprons. They swung enormous cleavers to hack up God knows what on the massive sacrificial alters of the chopping block tables. My instructions were: "Go right in. You won't be afraid. Just push your way up to the counter. Don't let anyone stop you. And tell the head butcher, the big one, tell him that if he doesn't take back this garbage and give you really A-1 meat, tell him your mother will come down there and hit him in the head with it."

It was not until I reached puberty that I was given assignments which would embarrass me more directly with regard to sexual role. I never did figure out whether or not these were contrived toughening-up exercises. Often I had to return a recent purchase to a department store's complaint department, usually a slip or a negligee of my mother's. By the time I was seventeen, I was able to go out to sell tough businessmen on the idea of buying space in the family-owned advertising directory. I didn't know I was supposed to be scared and so I did rather well.

For a long, long time I tried to figure out the rules about what was expected of me. The logic of it evaded me. It took many years for me to understand that it was not so much what I did, as whether or not it made my folks anxious. All the right-and-wrong kinds of issues were really reducible to whether or not their needs were being met.

To maintain their idealized view of their own characters, what they seemed to need most was someone else to blame. Even the simplest frustrations, of the sort which befall everyone, were given special meanings when they befell my parents. If a business deal did not work out the way my father had hoped it would, it was because he had been done in by the *Nahara*, the Evil Eye. When my mother went out shopping, and it rained *on her* (as though it did not rain on everyone), she would lament in Yiddish: "It's so hard to be a Jew." Often enough a bad-child-in-residence was explanation enough.

For thirteen years I was an only child, yet one who was constantly being compared with a large cast of super-numerary perfect siblings. What this amounted to was having all parental judgments, all reviews of my misbehavior contrasted with the wonderful performances of "all of the other fine Jewish boys in the neighborhood who you don't hear talking to their mothers that way."

By the time I was thirteen, old enough to have a Bar Mitzvah, my mother was pregnant. She waited until it was time for me to say, *"Today I am a man,"* before she was "in trouble." It was a time of many confusing fantasies for me. I became a man and my mother got pregnant. My first therapist and I later referred to my

Bar Mitzvah into manhood as "The time of the Great Lie."

I thought that my sister's entrance might save me from the constant barrage of criticism. And briefly it did. As instructed, in school I was smart and bad (A's in work, D's on conduct). That term I avoided suspension at school by telling my Junior High School Home Room teacher that my mother was pregnant. If he suspended me it would kill her and the baby too. He let me off with a warning. My sister was born in June of that term. It was the first time that no one asked to look at my report card. I was delighted (as well as scared to death, that now I *would* end up in prison someday, as they always said I would).

I felt off the spot. But I hated sharing the spotlight with Judy as well. All I could admit to was that baby-sitting her was a drag. My parents told me that I was mistaken. I enjoyed taking care of her, they explained, "because you love her." Later when she was old enough to join us at the table, they explained that I enjoyed having her take food from my plate "because she loves you."

Miscasting my sister as the flawless dream child was as burdensome for her as my playing the heavy was for me. She grew up painfully shy, filling her life for many years with secret fantasies lived out only in her immersion in reading books and pretending. Even through adolescense, a display cabinet of costumed dolls populated her isolated dream world.

By the time my sister was approaching puberty, I was gone. They began recasting her to take a revised version of my role. When I visited, my mother would tell me that somehow my wonderful darling of a sister was going to make trouble, she just knew it. "I thought boys were trouble," she would sigh, "but a girl can be more trouble." My sister hadn't yet reached puberty, and seemed in no way sexually precocious. My mother was aleady setting her up. "She's so pretty," my mother would complain. "Wait till the boys see her. I'll have to get her a pair of steel pants." She got a late start. She was not even told she was to be my understudy. My sister must be credited for doing what she could to fill the part of the delinquent child in my absence.

When I was young, abortions were criminal and dangerous. Pre-marital sex was not yet openly accepted. My unmarried teen-age sister confessed that she was pregnant and did not want to have the baby. The depth of my mother's concern was expressed in the delivery of one of her classic one-liners: "You certainly weren't thinking of me when you got yourself in all this trouble."

In my family, contradictory and confounding messages about the sexual scene were frequent. Again, the theme of children as trouble-makers was a recurring motif. Most warnings had to do with not getting a girl "in trouble." If so, I'd have to marry her, "for the sake of the children, God help them."

This all seemed particularly strange in the context of my mother's oft repeated line: "No woman but your Mother would put up with you." Then on to the tragedy of parenthood: "Small children bring small heartaches, big children (like you), big heartaches." She wanted very much that I should understand. "When you'll be a Mother," she would prophesize, "then you'll know." Her wishes for me in this regard: "You should live and be well, and they should tear your heart out, just like you tear out mine."

But all that would have to wait. For the moment, birth control was the issue. I remember so well the summer of my fifteenth year when I was finally old enough to get a job as busboy at a mountain resort. It was my first chance to escape for an entire summer. The night before I was to leave, my father took me aside. He told me that I would be meeting women at the resort, and that I should be prepared to act responsibly. He gave me a rubber and (more or less) told me how to use it.

I was still a virgin, excited and scared about beginning this aspect of my sexual career. I was deeply touched and felt lovingly supported by this gift from my father, by his acknowledging my manhood in so direct and helpful a way. After Labor Day I returned. Unfortunately I was still a virgin. But at least my father had acknowledged my manhood. He had given me a rubber. The day I returned, he asked for it back.

Sexual games with my mother invited more of an active contribution on my part. I remember that by the time I was sixteen (and no longer a virgin, thank God), I purchased my own rubbers.

One evening during that auspicious year, my mother was in the living room of our Bronx apartment playing Mah Jong with some of her women friends. I passed by on the way from my own room to the kitchen, and unintentionally overheard a fragment of their conversation. It seemed to be about sex, and so, of course, I hung around the hallway so that I could continue to listen surreptitiously.

One of the guests was expressing alarm at having found a rubber in the desk drawer of her young teen-age son. My mother was quick to reassure her, and to school her as to the advantage of her position. I heard my mother counsel: "Don't worry. They all do that. What do you expect? They get to be big boys. Even my Sheldon buys those. Better than he should get some girl in trouble and then God knows what. He keeps them in his dresser drawer. If you count them, and watch when he gets new boxes, then you can tell something about what's going one with them outside the house."

I knew then what I had to do. I bought a larger batch of rubbers than I had ever owned. Then I began putting them in the drawer and taking them out two or three at a time every few days. For weeks, I experienced secret glee as I watched the terror, the excitement, and the confusion on my mother's face. Needless to say, we never spoke about the matter.

It was not until some years later that there was to be one final oblique reference to such matters. I was about twenty-three, living most of the week in the Attendant's Home of the New Jersey State Mental Hospital at which I was interning as a clinical psychologist. I spent as much time as I could in New York at the apartment of a young woman with whom I was deeply involved.

I still needed to maintain my miscast role as inconsiderately demanding, but secretly loving dependent youth. Dutifully I returned to my parents' Bronx apartment weekly to drop off my dirty laundry. According to our script, they knew nothing about the women I dated. I had pretended to stop letting them know what was going on in my love-life years earlier. Following stage directions I began "secretly" taking out the non-Jewish girls who would some day deprive my parents of the *nachas* (earned blessings) of having wonderful Jewish grandchildren.

I never did figure out how I let them know whatever was required to cue them into treating me as badly as I insisted they did. All I know is that one Friday evening, this particular non-Jewish woman and I spent happily exploring the bookshops, coffe-houses, and bars of Greenwich village, finding the other colorfully misplaced young people who were our friends in those sad sweet years. It was much like other good evenings of those early months, with my ending up spending the rest of the weekend living at her apartment.

Too early on Saturday morning the phone rang. We woke to the nagging insistence of its summons. She fumbled sleepily for the receiver, and muttered an indistinct sound of greeting. Whatever she was hearing from the voice on the other end of the line snapped her harshly into a sudden and unsettled state of total wakefulness. The disturbing jangling of the phone had been so disruptively unnerving that perhaps I should not have been surprised when she handed my the receiver, saying: "It's for you. Someone who says she's your mother."

For a moment, I couldn't believe it either. But there she was on the phone, calling me at the apartment of a woman whom I believed she had never even heard of. She didn't give me a chance to say more than: "Mom, what are you calling me here for?"

She answered as though I were asking a stupid question the answer to which should have been obvious, even to me. She answered with loving contempt: "What am I calling you for? For what would a Mother be calling her son, when he's out all night, and she doesn't even know where he is if something should happen to her, God forbid? And when it's raining cats and dogs? I called you to tell you you shouldn't be there in all this rain without your *rubbers*. You don't know what you'll catch. Pneumonia, maybe. Your mother is calling you to remind you, you should take along your rubbers when you drop by at home to pick up your dirty laundry that your mother already washed for you."

Chapter II
Pretend You're Not Pretending

Over the years, by learning to pretend, I came to play my part well. I became the character I was miscast to be. I followed directions to become a bad boy, who did not express his feelings, and learned to make compromises. I went on to expand and overplay the part, making it into a neurotic caricature. Once I began to *pretend that I was not pretending*, I became an heroic exaggeration of what was required. My problems were elevated to self-destructively tragic proportions. I became Super-Bad, Super-Cool, and Super-Compromised.

Some of this was the result of what was laid on me by others, but much of my later needless suffering lay *not* in my problems, but in my solutions. As kids, we do what we can to survive our long period of relative helplessness. For some of us there is too much pressure to play a part someone else has cast us in. In some family settings no one cares enough to encourage us to find out who we might really be. Then there is no place to stand, no way to get perspective. To survive emotionally a child from such a home must take his own miscast role too seriously. He must learn to pretend he is not pretending.

A child trapped in a life of too much stress and too little caring has no power to change his situation, and no safe way to escape. To be fully aware of his profound helplessness and his vulnerability so early would be more than a child could bear. He needs to have at least the illusion of hope or he will drown in his despair. He must have something to believe in or he will be overwhelmed by panic. He must find some meaning in who he is or he will go mad.

How could he go on? If he realized then that there was no particular reason that he was not being cared for, nothing wrong with him that he could someday correct? How could he go on? Better to somehow find meaning in his suffering than to know that it is needless, senseless, unwarranted. Supposing at that point a kid was faced with understanding that he would have been treated differently if only he had been born next door, or in the house across the street? Any kid born in his house, at that time, and of that sex, would have been miscast as he was. No auditions would have been arranged. No try-outs were necessary. All the crazy demands, criticisms, and violations to which he is being subjected would have been laid on anyone appearing on stage at that point. What he has had to endure is meaningless. It has absolutely nothing to do with who he is, what he does, whether or not he is lovable, bright, and promising, or some kind of congenital loser.

Perhaps his first option is to learn to make his familiar suffering seem like an authentic and worthwhile part of himself.

Feeling bad gets to feel so natural to neurotics that all therapists sometimes hear patients complain of feeling uneasy when first experiencing improved emotional states. Having lived so long with anxiety, fear, and tension, a sense of well-being comes as an unsettlingly unfamiliar relief. To help bridge the gap, I sometimes share with such a patient a story which I heard comedian Buddy Hackett tell many years ago.

Buddy tells of growing up in a poor Jewish family on the lower East side of New York City. Somehow their poverty never resulted in any scarcity of food. Every day, at his mother's urging, he ate a bit more than he wanted of heavy, highly spiced, indigestibly fried Jewish meals.

At eighteen, Buddy was drafted into the Army. In Basic Training camp, he found himself in a new and "foreign" America. By the end of the second week, he woke up feeling very strange, vaguely ill, perhaps dying. Frightened and confused, he rushed to sick call clutching at his stomach. When asked what was wrong, all he could say was: "Doctor, my fire has gone out."

He had been away from home for two weeks, fourteen days of eating ordinary American Army chow. For the first time in his life, he did not have heartburn! This relief from discomfort was so unfamiliar that he was afraid that he was dying.

After learning to pretend he is not just playing a part a kid may next learn to glamorize his problems, by making them more interesting, dramatic, or colorful than his parents demand. In my own case, I went from bad boy to a marginally criminal teen-ager whose:

*flowers of evil blossomed in the fertile demi-monde
of drug addicts, fighting gangs, prostitutes, pimps,
and hustlers. I narrowly missed the abyss of heroin,
prison, and death by violence.* [1]

I went far beyond being just some inhibited kid who couldn't express his feelings. I became a Hipster, a Super-Cool stoic who was too much in the know to be caught up in the shallow emotional distress and enthusiasm of the square world. My disrespectfulness to my parents was exalted to a form a social rebelliousness. I graduated from fresh kid to the existential hero pose of agitating anarchist.

If all of these adaptations seem self-dramatizing, surely my compromising was the most theatrical of my solutions. At fifteen, I ran across a book called *Psychopathia Sexualis*, by a Dr. von Krafft-Ebing. [2] It was a turn-of-the-century medico-forensic, scientifically-pornographic study of a wide variety of sexual perversions. For me it was peculiarly a seductive book. Whenever the author would come to what I thought of as "the best parts," he would switch from English to Latin.

Fortunately I knew little Latin (and less Greek). As a result these untranslated sections gave my erotic imagination free rein. For a fifteen-year-old boy in the Forties this pseudo-scientific treatise was a truly wondrous volume. It described and diagnosed the acting out of every single one of my masturbatory fantasies. My parents had always wanted me to become a doctor when I grew up. For the first time, I agreed. It was then that I decided to study medicine. It was clear that I must become a psychiatrist so that I might cure all the poor souls who were given to acting out these terrible sexual perversions.

There had never been any question about whether or not I would attend college. This is how things stood. First I had to succeed in graduating from High School without going to Prison. Then even though I didn't deserve it, my parents would sacrifice and send me to college. When it was time to apply, I didn't know much more about going to college than that I was supposed to do so. No one bothered to try to help. I didn't even know I was allowed to ask for help. I just did what you do when you want to find a place that offers the services you are seeking. I looked up Colleges and Universities in the Yellow Pages. I applied to three New York City schools. Accepted by two of them, I chose to go to the closest one. That way I could save carfare, get to the neighborhood poolroom when I had a free hour, and continue to complain that I had to go on living at home.

After a year or so of pre-med immersion in physical science courses, I knew that four years in Medical School would destroy my mind. I asked around and found out that I could become a Clinical Psychologist instead of a Psychiatrist. I would be able to study the Social Sciences and Philosophy instead and still learn to cure Sexual Perverts. I went home and had a long talk with my folks. It was the first time I had approached them for help with a personal problem since I was a little kid. I told them of my career conflict, my uncertainty about making the switch, the personal identity crisis I felt I was going through. They listened without speaking. Finally my father nodded deferentially to my mother. She took the cue and asked just one question: "Will they still call you 'Doctor'?" I assured her "they" would. "So what's the big problem?" she summarized.

It was "Go to Prison" or "Become a Doctor!" I did both. I became a Prison Doctor. My parents were proud that I was a doctor but ashamed of the class of people I associated with in my work. I was finally a doctor, but I still hung around with bums. To concretize the problem, I dedicated my Doctoral Dissertation to my folks. I even gave them a copy for their living-room coffee-table. It was based on unexpurgated interviews with psychotic patients (expletives *un*deleted). My Father said, "Whoever heard of a dirty thesis, before? Who could we show it to without exposing your shame?"

I got to meet all the sexual perverts I hoped to meet in my work at the Building for the Criminally Insane. I have written elsewhere[3] of how much more they were able to do to help me with my problems, than I was to help them with theirs.

.   .   .   .

A child who grows up in a family situation in which there is a great deal of miscasting will have to at least pretend to play his designated part just to survive the period of his helpless dependence on the family. Under certain circumstances he may emerge from the family production chronically cast as a tragic hero. By learning to pretend that he is not pretending, he may extend his role to the needless suffering of developing a neurotic character style. Such a role will make his plot line certain and his part dramatic. The price to be paid for taking himself too seriously will be hysterically exaggerated misery, obsessively boring redundancy, and compulsively rigid predicatability. Type-cast neurotics seem very much like one another to me. It is only as they are able to give up these parts and reveal themselves that they seem more genuine, interesting, and excitingly different from one another.

In order to better understand the contribution of *Miscasting* to the development of Neurosis, I would like to compare it to the *Double Bind* and its contribution to the development of schizophrenic symptoms in a person caught up in that sort of destructive family situation. The necessary ingredients for a double bind situation are:

1. *Two or more persons* . . . (in which) the double bind situation is inflicted on the 'victim' by mother alone or by some combination of mother, father, and/or siblings.

2. *Repeated experience* . . . (so much that it) comes to be an habitual expectation.

3. *A primary negative injunction* . . . This may have either of two forms (a) 'Do not do so and so, or I will punish you,' or (b) 'If you do not do so and so, I will punish you.' Learning based on avoidance of punishment may be either the withdrawal of love or the expression of hate or anger—or most devastating—(a) kind of abandonment . . . (The result is chronic fear).

4. *A secondary injunction conflicting with the first at a more abstract level, and like the first enforced by punishments or signals which threaten survival* . . . for example 'Do not see this as punishment'; 'Do not see me as the punishing agent'; 'Do not think of what you must not do' . . .

5. *A tertiary negative injunction prohibiting the victim from escaping from the field.*

6. Finally, the complete set of ingredients is no longer necessary when the victim has learned to perceive his universe in double bind patterns.

necessary when the victim has learned to perceive his universe in double bind patterns.[4]

Stuck in a situation in which whatever he chooses to do or not do will be punished, the victim learns to act in crazy ways. These unconventional ways of communicating become the only seemingly "sensible" ways to resond appropriately to an overwhelmingly insoluble, survival-threatening, seemingly inescapable plight. The experience of this spider-web of a trap, generates intolerably terrifying anxiety, and offers no "reality-oriented" options.

A clinical illustration of the anguish of the double-bind no-win situation and the "crazy" behavior it can generate is described by Gregory Bateson in this way:

> . . . A young man who had fairly well recovered from an acute schizophrenic episode was visited in the hospital by his mother. He was glad to see her and impulsively put his arm around her shoulders, whereupon she stiffened. He withdrew his arm and she asked, "Don't you love me anymore?" He then blushed, and she said, "Dear, you must not be so easily embarrassed and afraid of your feelings." The patient was able to stay with her only a few minutes more and following her departure he assaulted an aide and was put in the tubs.[5]

That, then is a schematic description of the Double Bind and an illustration of its contribution to the development of schizophrenic symptoms (in this case an irrational outburst of murderous rage which the patient would later "explain" on a delusional basis). How does this contrast with Miscasting and its contribution to the development of neurotic style?

In order to compare the two destructive situations and their outcomes, let us consider using descriptive criteria for the Miscasting configuration which parallel Bateson's schematic analysis of the Double Bind. The necessary criteria for a Miscasting situation then would be:

1. *Two or more persons* in which the miscasting is imposed on the child by the parents, with siblings sometimes making a contribution.

2. *Repeated experiences* under so much stress and with so little supportive caring that it becomes an habitual expectation.

3. *A primary positive injunction.* This may have either of two forms: (a) 'If only you will pretend to be who I say I need you to be, I will reward you,' or (b) 'If only you will stop pretending to be the person you feel you are, I will reward you.' Learning based on seeking far distant future rewards. These include a happy ending, rave reviews, or ultimate stardom. The resultant feelings are a chronic sense of guilt and inadequacy.

4. *A secondary injunction conflicting with the first but at a less explicit level, reinforced by small immediate subtle rewards* (such as a masked smile, wink, or pat). This may have either of two forms: (a) 'Do not ever feel satisfied that you have succeeded in becoming the person I want you to pretend to be,' or (b) 'Pretend that you cannot help doing some of the things I say I want you to stop doing.'

5. *A tertiary negative injunction prohibiting the victim from gaining any perspective, best stated as:* 'Pretend that you are not pretending.'

6. Finally, the complete set of ingredients is no longer necessary when the victim has learned to perceive his universe in theatrical Miscasting patterns.

Stuck in a situation in which he has to take seriously things he knows are not true, in which he will not only be rewarded for performances which are somehow not quite right, the victim learns to act out his miscast part. He comes to feel that there is a special mission for him in life, and that his suffering is somehow worthwhile. It is as though he acts out of some tragic necessity, whether it be with regard to the neurotic symptoms (which he cannot help) or the neurotic character style (which involves getting his own way with him). Thus one aspect of his heroic posture is that of exaggerated self-importance and indulgent spitefulness. Yet, paradoxically, anotehr resultant motif is his sense of being driven to do what he feels he must do, so that he is very hard on himself, never being fully satisfied with his performance, rarely free to improvise.

Another illustration of my own miscasting occurred around the issue of mastery of the world of physical objects. Early on I was billed as the achieving intellectual who would some day make my parents happy. They were careful to see to it that I didn't confuse the plot line by learning to use the wrong props. Whenever I picked up a tool, I was immediately subjected to the clear and harsh stage direction: "Put down that hammer. Do you want to hurt yourself? Go get a book."

Repeated criticisms stifled my curiosity about building things, as well as making me feel painfully unconfident in dealing with even the simplest aspects of the physical world. Soon, it began to be pointed out again and again how coarse and clumsy I was. The term for me at such awkward moments was "Clumsy ox." If only I really loved them . . . if only I really wanted to be a good boy . . . if only I really tried, then I could be careful and competent. And "stop walking into walls."

I grew so tense about trying to stop being such a lout, that of course I became clumsier and clumsier. I was forever knocking over glasses of milk at dinner, bumping into things, stumbling and fumbling through life. They said: "A great horse like you breaks everything he touches." I tried to do as they directed. Each time I did, one of them would smile with satisfaction and say, "You see, what did I tell you!"

Eventually, it became a matter of my own pride. I began to view myself as "an intellectual," too cerebral to bother with everyday dealings with the material world of mere things. No longer simply "the fat kid with glasses who couldn't catch a ball," I began insisting I was really too sensitive to waste myself on anything as shallow as sports.

In the earlier illustration, the young schizophrenic man resorted to crazy assaultive behavior to deal with the over-whelming helplessness he felt before his mother's masterful double bind. His over-training and intense dependency prevented him from stepping back and commenting on his mother's pathologi-cally communicative behavior in a way which might have obviated his need to act crazy instead. The schizophrenic behavior could have been avoided, if he had been able to say:

> Mother, it is obvious that you become uncomfrotable when I put my arm around you, and that you have difficulty accept-ing a gesture of affection from me.[6]

The sane way out of the double bind requires that the "victim" be able to recognize that he is helpless to respond correctly to one injunction without being punished for violating the other. Once able to correct his discrimination of what order of message to respond to, he then can make a metacommunicative statement. That is, he can comment on what kind of position mother is putting him in, without being bound to play this no-win game on her terms.

The schizophrenic needs to solve this double bind problem by getting past the disordered thinking which results from repeated entrappment in these deadly, obscure double messages. In contrast, the neurotic's resolution to his miscasting lies in his learning to discriminate between pretending and the spontaneous expressing of feeling. He must learn to be *irreverent* enough to realize that he and his parents are simply ordinary people, people who make mistakes, people who act foolish from time to time, ordinary people just like everybody else. This requires his choosing comedy over tragedy, and the *holy* insecurity of irreverence over a search for higher principles. It also requires some acceptance of the absurdity of life over a demand for Deeper Meaning or a Grand Design. Most of all it requires that he stop taking himself so damn seriously.

To illustrate this, I return to my role as The Clumsy One.

After years as a non-builder, I married, and was encouraged by my wife to redefine my own role. I found that I *could* learn to use tools, not only without hurting myself, but with great competence and satisfaction. From the beginning of our relationship there has been one aspect of our exchanges which I have particularly valued. It is our encouraging one another to discover what each would really like to do, but never before dared to imagine was possible.

Following several modest carpentry ventures in rented homes, I undertook to shape our lives with my own hands in the first home which we came to own. I built boldly. Integrating the scholarly role into which my parents had put me, with the physical creativeness encouraged by my wife, I built great, bold, natural wood, floor-to-ceiling bookcases in our living room and study.

My parents were coming to visit. I let myself forget that I could no longer get confirmation from them. I was filled with pride of the bookish child grown into the artisan man. I wanted my parents to see my bookcases, to see whom I had become. They arrived for their visit early one Saturday morning.

As soon as I could I had them in the living room standing before this eighth wonder. "How do you like it," I demanded. For once my parents both agreed, "They're really very, very nice." My mother: "Who did you get to build them?" My father: "And how much did they cost?" I, in righteous indignation, "I built them myself with these two hands, these hands that you taught me could only turn pages. I bought the wood and the stain for very little money, and I built them myself, all by myself."

Pause, silence. I hoped that they were embarrassed, or ashamed, sorry about how badly they had miscast me. My mother ad-libbed: "Bastard, how come you never built bookcases for me?" And I, right back, laughing: "And then you would have let me be a good boy, right?"

Comic relief and freedom from miscasting can be supplied by any of the central characters. It may be not the neurotic-victim-son but the parents who change first.

One of the pivotal scenes in the gradual revision of the flawed tragedy in which my parents and I had been for so long stuck in reruns, occurred when my first article appeared in print. I was pleased and excited over this achievement and recognition. I had ordered reprints and was about to mail them out (to almost anyone who would be willing to receive one). My parents were coming to visit us on the farm in New Jersey in which we had come to live so happily. My parents, who could live comfortably in a regularly burglarized apartment building, had let us know that they were tense and anxious about coming to visit us "in the country" where familiar muggers were replaced by great strange beasts, such as cows and chickens. When I grew up, trees were surrounded by small fences lest they break loose and run wild.

My own growing apprehension, however, was not tied to a change of setting for my parents. They'd fuss, they'd be somewhat insulting, they'd be funny, it would get straightened out. My anxiety lay elsewhere. I found that I very much wanted to give my parents a copy of this first reprint, the picture of my first brainchild. But as I imagined doing so, I found that I balked irritably. I didn't want to be exploited any more. This was mine

and I wanted them to respond to it because they loved *me*—
because they would be happy because I was happy.

My father turned toward my mother, looking for a cue line,
trying to find out how he should respond. My mother hardly
hesitated a moment before she set up another of her
show-stopping one-liners: "You want to know which it'll be: You
want to know whether I'll be happy for you or happy for me?
Wait, I'll tell you." She paused a single dramatic moment. With an
uncharacteristically warm yet mischievous smile she focused the
whole cast and audience on her reply. "The answer is *both*, of
course!"

. . . .

I have contrasted the destructive family patterns of the
schizophrenic-producing double bind with those of the neurotic
style engendering miscastings. I do not mean to give the impression
that anyone who is raised confronted with the one may not also at
times be subjected to the other. There are lots of different kinds of
troubles in this life. Having one kind does not necessary protect
any of us from suffering other kinds as well.

I remember one dramatic admixture which my patients and I
encountered in each other during a recent group therapy session. It
had been a long lousy day. I was tired and working on my second
headache. This one had lasted for four hours and I still had some
residual pain as I entered the group therapy session. Thank God, it
was my last appointment of the day.

As the group settled into their traditional brief opening
silence, I noticed that Peter looked like warmed-over death. He
rolled his eyes and lolled his head, while his usually petulant
mouth hung open as though beyond caring. Outside of the group,
Peter was an unhappily married clinical psychologist. During the
group sessions, he usually held the voluntary/appointed office of
the nice-guy-who-tries-so-hard-he-always-antagonizes-everyone
(cum chronic complainer).

Today he had promoted himself to the starring role of group
madman. His clinical experience had served to refine the excellent
training which his psychotic mother had long ago provided. Some

good soul made the mistake of asking him what was wrong. Suddenly all of his considerable stage presence was turned on as he dramatically moaned about his head being all mixed up. He complained: "My mind is blocked, there's a suffocating pressure in my chest, I feel that my genitals have disappeared, and that my body is turning inside out, like my asshole is open and everyone can hurt me."

The group seemed appalled and frightened. Some members inquired sympathetically about his condition, and received more roccoco lunacy for their trouble.

He turned pathetically to me, whining: "Shelly, won't you please help me."

I'd had it for the day. "Can it, Peter," I blasted. "I've had a headache for the past four hours. I don't need any of your shit on top of that. Now you either talk about what's going on in your life and deal, or take your ass over to St. Elizabeth's Hospital and spend the rest of your miserable days in that human warehouse pouting with the rest of those stubborn looneys. If you want to play schiophrenia, go do it somewhere else."

Peter was quiet, but suddenly seemed clearer and more alert. He began to talk about his unfinished fight with his wife, and his messed up relations on the job. The group joined in and some things got a bit straighter for him.

At the end of the hour, he smiled warmly at me saying, "thanks for curing my psychosis."

"That was easy," I answered. "Now if only I could cure your neurosis . . . and my headaches."

Chapter III
Irreverent Metatheater

The tragic figure with whom the neurotic identifies has a long and proud theatrical history. Beginning as the protagonist of classical Greek drama, the victim of tragedy is more than merely the unfortunate hero of a story with an unhappy ending. Antigone, Oedipus, and Orestes each suffered from a tragic flaw of character, from some classically "admirable" trait. Each fell victim to some unyieldingly implacable principle. In the end each was thrown by the weight of his or her own pretension. Such a change of fortune is always ironic. The resultant misery is always emotionally overwhelming. The final disaster always a willful waste of life's possibilities.

But beginning with Shakespeare's *Hamlet*, an important change in Western dramaturgy came about. Hamlet is the first significant hero of what Lionel Abel has called Metatheater.[1] In the metaplay, as in psychotherapy, the primary characteristic is the self-consciousness of the dramatist (or therapist) himself, and then of the protagonists (or patients). Like Hamlet, the psychotherapy patient is no longer Fate's pawn, but the aware shaper of his own destiny.

In addition to the new self-consciousness, both metatheater and psychotherapy provide a skeptical imagination which regards all inexorable values as false. Everything is open to question. Subjective-consciousness' gain becomes the "objective" world's loss. Fantasy becomes inseparable from the reality it infuses.

Both metatheater and psychotherapy come beyond tragedy. Each elevates imagination above circumstance, and destiny above fate. Each underscores hope without perfection, safety without certainty, and responsibility without blame.

The death of tragedy has come about through changes in Western imagination which have been explored in depth elsewhere (by Kaufmann,[2] by Steiner,[3] and by Abel[4]). I shall only point to some of the crucial parameters of this evolving European-American outlook on life, without presuming to explain them.

It took centuries for the Western view to emerge from the heroic vision of the ancient Greeks.

This was by no means the case with the Oriental perspective. The Eastern view of life as suffering, with the inevitability of man's ultimate defeat and death has never been a tragic vision. From an Oriental vantage point, "nobility of spirit" is no more than an illusion. It is no more than a man's being trapped by desire, by his foolishly willful struggle to change that which he cannot change. In fact all need not be changed for him to be able to find peace. The tragic preoccupation only serves to rob man of the immediacy of his participation in the playfulness of life. His unwillingness to surrender his willful Self merely chains him to the needless pain of existence.

The death of tragedy begins with man's self-conscious recognition of his conflicts and imperfections. He can only know his options by facing his helplessness. Just as important is his skepticism, his questioning of implacable values and higher purposes.

The majestic sadness of tragedy has given way to pathetic everyday unhappiness in a world which God has abandoned to the vulnerability of ordinary man's splintered consciousness. Only neurosis restores needless tragic suffering to those unfortunate enough to be so miscast.

A comparison of tragedy and metatheater will help clarify some crucial differences. It illuminates the contrast between neurotic heroic life style and the uncertain, ambiguous way of the ordinary man who does not overdramatize his life. Tragedy has God as its principal spectator, while metatheater is a matter of living in the moment for one's own sake. Tragedy occurs against a back-drop of ultimate order, while in metatheater, order is something which men must continually improvise. Tragedy glorifies a strong sense of the external reality of the unchanging world, while metatheater intends the world as a projection of human consciousness. It is a world in flux, experienced differently by different people. Every experience can be genuine, and no one image of the world is ultimate. Nothing is beyond question!

Tragedy insists on a fixed reality in which human existence is subservient to Fate. In metatheater, fate can be transformed into personal destiny by imaginative acceptance of the life we find ourselves cast in. No one's life is so really different from that of all the other ordinary people.

The seeming validity of the tragic vision is eroded by the Death of God. If God is *not* dead, He has certainly grown weary of man's nonsense, and fed up with his arrogance. He has left man to his own devices in a world without order, empty of higher purposes. There is a medieval parable which tells that:

> In some obscure village in central Poland, there was a small synagogue. One night, when making his round, the Rabbi entered and saw God sitting in a dark corner. He fell upon his face and cried out: "Lord God, what art Thou doing here?" God answered him with a small voice: "I am tired, Rabbi, I am tired unto death."[5]

Tragedy requires the burdensome presence of God in the world. If His shadow no longer falls upon us, we cannot be truly tragic figures. And in such a natural world, in a world without higher purpose, without Justice or Mercy, human imperfection sets the only standards available—ambiguous, error-laden, absurd as they may be.

In the post-tragic world of ordinary existence, there are only common men speaking prose. It is only in the world of high tragedy that:

> *Kings, prophets, and heroes speak in verse,*
> *thus showing that the exemplary personages in*
> *the commonwealth communicate in a manner nobler*
> *and more ancient than that reserved to common men.*[6]

> *When men speak verse, they are not prone to*
> *catching colds or suffering from indigestion.*
> *. . . If there are bathrooms in the house of*
> *tragedy, they are for Agamemmnon to be murdered in.*[7]

*In tragedy, we do not observe men eating, nor
do we hear them snore.*[8]

But like it or not, in the post-tragic natural humanistic world, men
fart, fool around, and fuck up—and ladies do too.

Each family in which children are raised is simply another
example of this unremarkably imperfect life. My own family is
certainly as ordinary as everyone else's and I try where I can to
resist the temptation to make it into something theatrically special.
It is only to the extent that we can live in the irreverent
metatheater mode, and lead unheroic lives that we may avoid the
needless suffering of noble tragedy.

You can be sure that I lay some bad trips on my kids. Of
course, I am tempted to give them the good stuff that my folks
didn't give to me, and to save them from the bad stuff that they
dumped on my innocent child's head. Certainly I give way to
using and abusing my kids, because they are little and I am big,
because they are dependent and I am in charge, because it is easier
than dealing directly with my wife. At times I subject them to
miscasting, double binds, and all kinds of other crap.

In the many ways I have not fucked them over, what
worthwhile aspects of our interactions protect them from
becoming as tragically unhappy as I have been? I am presuming
here that though each clearly has his own kinds of hang-ups, none
of my kids is as far gone as I was as a teenager. And too for the
moment I am not focussing on how much their well-being is
simply the product of what my wife has given them. These issues
aside, part of what has been nurturant is an atmosphere in which
we have been concerned not to ask too much of them, in the sense
of trying not to ask *them* to take care of *us*. Parents are supposed
to take care of kids. Not the other way around. A basic premise of
mine, one which to me needs no justification and therefore
probably has an instinctual basis is: *Kids are entitled.*

Each kid is entitled to have a sense that his parents are saying
to him: "You're my kid, and I love you very much. I want us to get
to really know one another. I will take care of you. We'll try to
understand what you are feeling, to find out what you need to

make you happy, and help you to learn how to find that happy space for yourself." Of course, some aspects of the message change as the child grows older. Gradually his increasing independence must be supported as you move toward separating, toward giving each other up so that each will have a life that is really his own.

These matters are very complex. The struggle to be the sort of parent my kids seem to need sometimes seems overwhelming. It is in that aspect of my life which is devoted to being a parent that I most often fail. Still much of it is so good that I have no question anymore about the worth of such a trip for myself, of its lovely (though often painful) place in my own life.

For now, however, I wish to focus attention on a single aspect of parental attitudes which may save a child from a costly commitment to a neurotic life style. I believe the crucial issue is that of *Irreverence.* As the father, I take care of the kids in some ways, and must command some respect for my authority in order to do so. But that authority must be grounded in my children's experience-based trust that at least for for the most part, I am operating in good faith and with good judgment.

But this trust must be tempered by the recognition that sometimes I may unwittingly be exploiting them, or at the very least that I make many mistakes. No matter how good my judgment may be, I can certainly be counted on to act foolishly from time to time.

Therefore, the kids must be taught that nothing I say or do is sacred. There is nothing too serious to be kidded about. A playful attitude needs to be developed. It must poke through pretense without hurtng the other any more than is absolutely required. Hopefully this will not only allow them (and me) to survive their growing up. It will be useful outside the home as well. If this sort of Irreverence is carefully nurtured it will provide support for their freedom when faced with arbitrary authority wherever they may encounter it. At the very least it serves as a vehicle for a great deal of good-humored kidding and playing around. But most of all it helps each of us to learn not to take himself too seriously.

It's not so easy to be a child. In a sense:

> . . . any son (is) forced to be an actor in his parents' script.
> They chide him, spank him, dress him, coddle him, order
> him around: to be a child means to take direction.[9]

Still, parental responsibility can be maintained for a small child's welfare without imposing an arbitrary, unquestioned oppressive authority on the beleaguered youngster. What then are the outside limits of the parents' rights and responsibilities in directing their children's lives? What are the children's rights to challenge the roles their parents take and impose, in the interests of avoiding being miscast into lives of tragedy?

This is hazardous territory, an area between parent and child in which feelings are easily hurt, and destructively angry exchanges are ready temptation. Some of this cannot be avoided, but it sure helps to approach such sensitive places with humor, with a feeling for the comic aspects of being human.

Laughter is the sound of freedom. Life is for me far more a comedy than a tragedy. Nothing should be so serious that we are not allowed to have fun about it. There is a story I sometimes tell my patients to help support their Irreverence for my therapeutic authority, my parental transference, my Grand Guruship.

> The story is about God and St. Peter going out to play golf together one Sunday afternoon after church. God teed up on the first hole, swung his driver mightily, and sliced the ball off into the rough beside the fairway. Just as the ball hit the ground, a rabbit came running out from beneath a bush, picked up God's golf ball in his mouth, and ran with it out onto the fairway. Down from the sky swooped a hawk and pounced on the rabbit. The hawk picked up the rabbit in its claws, and flew with it over the green. A hunter spotted the hawk, took aim with his rifle, and shot the bird in midflight. The hawk dropped the rabbit onto the green. The golfball fell from the rabbit's mouth and rolled into the cup for a hole-in-one.
>
> Peter turned to God with exasperation, saying: "Come on now. Do you want to play golf, or do you want to fuck around?"

At my best, that is, when I am feeling best about myself, there is no aspect of my parental authority that it is not all right for my children to kid about. There are no Truths which are above being questioned, and no rules which cannot be broken. Still as a family, we are not simply a group of children at play. I am supposed to know something about what I am up to, to take some responsibility for being in charge. I must bring to bear whatever wisdom and experience provides to do the best job I can to see that the playfulness does not reach destructive proportions.

I wrote earlier that it's not so easy to be a child. It's not so easy to be a parent either. The same metatheatrical paradox to be found in a post-tragic role of being a father must be met in being a contemporary therapist as well. Doing therapy, like parenting requires continuous playful innovation. Ad libbing my way through a world in flux, again and again having to reconcile the polarities of responsibility and freedom, I encourage the same sort of playful irreverence in my patients as I do in my kids.

When it feels as though a patient's playfulness is threatening to lead us to destructive places, I get scared, and if he can get past his excitement, he does too. As a reassuring comfort to both of us, I often interrupt at this point to tell the story of Dr. Smartass. It begins:

> Once upon a time there were two young men who became close friends. While sitting and talking at lunch one day, much to their surprise they discovered that they were both in treatment with the same psychotherapist. As they compared notes, they agreed that the doctor was competent and helpful. He was also maddeningly composed and pompously sure of himself. If only there was some way to shake him up, to make him feel as unsettled as he made them feel.
>
> Gleefully they hit upon a scheme to unhorse the good doctor. Together they made up an elaborate dream, rehearsing the telling of it until each could present it as his own. That Monday would be the day of reckoning. The first young man would go in for his appointment in the morning and tell the therapist "his" dream. His friend would repeat the performance in his own session that same afternoon. Let's see how Doctor Smartass would handle that one.
>
> On Monday the first young man went to his session, told his carefully rehearsed dream. He hid his secret glee as he and the therapist worked on interpreting the dream. That afternoon, his friend gave a brilliant straight-faced performance, as he too recounted the dream as if it were his own. Every detail of the second telling was the same as the first.
>
> He was delighted to see an uncharacteristic look of bewilderment come across the therapist's face. "God, that's strange," said the doctor. "That's the *third* time today I've heard that exact same dream."

Living in a world beyond tragedy, in a world of metatheater, means living in a world without God, a world without appeal. In such a world, there are no heroes and heroines, no special people. The motto of the Moscow Art Theatre tells us: "There are no small roles—only small actors.[10] One has the opportunity to play the father or the therapist or the candlestick-maker. This requires the willingness to give all of yourself to it though you recognize it is no more and no less important than any other part. It means learning to improvise, make mistakes, feel the freedom and the excitement of making it up as you go along as very best you can.

The Hell of it is, there's no way to be sure no matter what you do. You have to figure it out as best you can, know what you feel, say what you mean, and do what you say. You have to risk being the fool (again), take your best shot, hope it works, and forgive yourself if it doesn't. Who knows what's allowed anyway?

In re-examining their lives in the course of undergong psychotherapy many patients are faced with once more evaluating the shoulds and should-nots which they have incorporated from parents, institutions, and community during the course of their growing up. Taking personal responsibility as an adult for deciding what is allowed and what is not is usually a painful, at times a comic struggle.

There is a story I sometimes tell to offer a foretaste of the Day of Judgment:

> The time is the not too distant future. We have finally destroyed ourselves by means of a nuclear holocaust. Everyone is waiting restlessly in a seemingly endless line leading up to the Gates of Heaven. At the head of the line, Peter is deciding which souls shall enter and which shall be turned away.
>
> Some distance from the Gates, an American stands in line wringing his hands in apprehension. Suddenly he hears a murmur beginning at the front of the line, and growing into a joyful rush of sound as it builds in volume moving down the line toward his place. He can make out sounds of celebration in many languages. He hears shouts of "Bravo," "Bravissimo," "Bis," "Encore," and "Hip, Hip Hooray."

"What is it? What's it all about?" he implores of those up ahead of him on the line. At last someone closer to the Gates shouts back to him, "Peter just told us: 'Screwin' don't count!'"

If this is the way it is, if nobody knows for sure what is right and what is wrong, we'd each best be free of unearned respect for authority. It may be useful in some cases to have someone in charge, whether it be a parent for kids, an elected president for the nation's citizens, or an alternating "dance-master" for facilitating the distribution of daily chores for members of a hippie-commune. But this person-in-charge must never become more than an ordinary human being who is temporarily serving a function of leadership for the group.

Because of human dependency, or transference reactions, reinforced by the archetypal role and perhaps the personal charisma of a particular leader, we will all be tempted again and again to cast the authority into the hero-role. We will be tempted to see him as bigger, stronger, wiser, more reliable than any of us who depend on him. A piece of our own worth may be sacrificed to his image so that we can have the perfect parent to take care of us.

There is not way to get past such hazardous temptations once and for all. The wish to be taken care of never dies, nor does the wish to at least find the perfect leader, if we cannot ourselves become the culture hero. The best protection is Irreverence, the freedom from taking anything or anyone too seriously. My kids were quick to develop a flair for a kind of self-affirming irreverence. This attitude has protected them. It has helped keep me from being any more crazy than I absolutely have to be. Best of all it has added warmth and humor to all of our lives.

I remember one early expression of their irreverent insistence on determining the nature of reality from their own personal experience rather than on the basis of any parental injunctions. David, our middle child, was about six years old at the time, and our youngest Nick, (then Nicky) was about four. I was deeply immersed in the tension-filled transformation from clumsy ox to carpenter. Nick was watching wide-eyed as I measuerd, sawed, and put up the bookcase shelves.

David entered the room and sized up the siatuation in an instant. He quickly took Nick by the hand and led him away. As he rescued Nick, David counselled him: "Hey, you crazy or something, standing so close when Dad's building shelves. Don't you know he's gonna hit his thumb with that hammer? And when he does he's gonna turn around and holler at any kid who's around just like it was your fault."

They soon developed a grab-bag of such vignettes. They had fun banding together to support the independence of each one's confidence in his own judgment when faced with the arbitrariness of my authority. It also gave them a store of precedents to cite when any new omniscience on my part needed deflating. Nick's favorite has always been: "Don't forget the time when we were all little and you told us, 'Daddy's very, very tired this evening, so *you kids* will have to go to bed early.'"

Sometimes their irreverence is expressed with irritation rather than good humor. At such times I believe they simply feel hopeless about being able to instruct me in not taking myself too seriously. I remember one time asking Nick to do some chore, when he was quite young. He told me he didn't want to do it. At that point, playing the wise, fully rational father, I took time out to say: "I want to discuss this with you. Now just listen and Daddy will explain why you should do this." He shook his head, interrupting my speech with exasperation: "Don't explain. I'll do it, I'll do it. Just don't explain any more."

At other times their approach is one of straight-faced broad satire. The example that comes to mind is out of a time when I was into laying on them some kind of super-integrity responsibility trip. In the manner of an inexperienced Gestalt therapist I was into correcting their way of saying things so that they would become more actively in charge of their lives. It was typical enlightened nonsense of insisting they say "I won't" instead of saying "I can't." I'd get them to stop and reconstruct crucial sentences from a passive to an active mode. A kid would say, "My milk spilled," and sanctimoniously I would correct him, so that he could say it right: "*I* spilled the milk." I wanted to "help" the kids to get past having things simply happen to them. I tried to get them to speak, think, and feel in active, here-and-now terms in which they would take full responsibility for their actions.

They were quick to pick up this mannered style of speaking (they intuitively knew that thinking and feelng that nonsense would have made them sick). They pretended to go along until they felt I was ready to be cut down to life size. Each of the three dutifully corrected "my bike broke," to "I broke my bike," "My Math book is lost," to "I lost my Math book," and so on. This went on for weeks until one day, David came in from the yard soaking wet from a sudden downpour of rain. He must have seen on my face some readiness to blame him. "I was just going to tell you, Dad," he said in a rush. "I'm sorry, I guess I rained all over myself." That line effectively ended another miscasting routine I had worked out for my kids.

The best lines and most touching interactions with our oldest son, Jon, came when he became the consummate Seventies teenager. At this writing he is the only one of the three who has left home, though David is on the threshhold of leaving for college as well. So it is that the scenes featuring Jon pivot on our jousting over our equivalence as full-fledged men.

Any prop will do for an improvised skit. This time it was my smoking gear. I love smoking a pipe, one of the many props of my guruship, but it entails carrying about a great deal of equipment. One Saturday afternoon at the pipe and tobacco shop, I noticed that there were some hand-made leather handbags hanging on display on a rack alongside of the carved meerschaum pipes. I asked about the bags and learned that the tobacconist's sister had made them. When she came out of her workshop at the back of the store, she turned out to be a young attractive, near-hippie crafts-person type. She was pleasantly responsive to my enquiries about the possibility of her tailoring a bag to my needs. I wanted to be more comfortably able to carry my pipes, tobacco, and smoking tools wherever I went. The deal was quickly set and two weeks later I had my own hand-crafted, dark richly tooled leather shoulder-strap pouch of a handbag.

I showed it to my oldest son, Jon, he of the shoulder length hair and one gold earring. He liked the bag, and it was clear that he liked my freedom to purchase and carry this traditionally female device. However, he could not resist underlining our generational differences, by asking, "Are you sure you're comfortable carrying it?" Half-kidding, I responded, "Yes, except when your mother refers to it as my *purse*. Jon brightened at once. "See," he smiled, "You're still stuck with some of your sexist hangups."

I could see that we had arranged this schism by unspoken mutual accord. The lines were drawn. It was not necessary to fight it out. And so I answered with patriarchal condescension, "I guess you just don't have a sense of humor about some things *yet*."

Jon answered with all the confident superiority of youth, "About some things I guess I'll never *need* a sense of humor."

Obviously one of us has a lot to learn yet. But in some instances it is clear that we have each learned a great deal from one another. A touchingly lovely illustration of this occurred recently. Jon had called to let us know that he would have a few weeks off between college terms and that he planned to get a temporary job here in Washington during that time. To make clear the uncertainty about our relationship during this phase of its transition, he asked, "Can I stay at your house?" From our point of view, he still lives there, and so of course we agreed.

Having him back home felt good, but we were all careful to keep it as awkward as we needed it to be. For his part, Jon met his mother's efforts to feed him in the old ways by asserting his serious new-found vegetarian mode. It took a while for them to enjoy exchanging organic recipes and cooking together.

He reminded me of where we stood right off. The very first night (and many nights thereafter) he arranged to sleep away from home at a neighboring friend's communal living situation. Only slowly did we transform this needed distance into grounds for serious personal exchanges about just where he and I stand on different ways in which a man might live meaningfully.

There was of course much tenderness, good and loving talk, and raucous playfulness (flavored at times with some of Jon's residual boyishness). But the defining of his manly separate ways was the baseline of most exchanges. I in turn wrestled with my own confusion about when to try to be his father and when to enjoy being his friend.

Our loving struggle was revealed in one dining-room exchange. We have a large family table with five chairs to accommodate my wife, my three sons, and myself. These consist of one captain's chair and four mate's chairs. The captain's chair is (of course) my seat. That evening I reached the talbe to discover that my youngest son, Nick, had taken the captain's chair to his own place (his chair being in need of repair). I half-kidded, half-chided him about taking my chair. Nick complained that my playing out the father thing about the chair was unfair.

Jon immediately went to the barricades. Striking a Maoist posture, he challenged my commitment to what he saw as being empty traditional rituals. He exposed them as being aimed at oppressing the powerless minority constituted by my sons. I countered by claiming that my having the captain's chair was not really crucial. Any place that I sat would automatically become the head of the table.

Jon said that was just me at my worst, an attitude he's known over a long period of time. He pointed out its irrational origins in my insisting that my sons call me "Dad" rather than "Shelly." I explained that that particular ritualistically deferential gesture was really a family safeguard. Its implied reciprocities of responsibility had protected my children from my brutality when they were small. Now it would protect me from the homicidal menace of their primal horde now that they were big enough to do me in. This seemed to Jon merely a rationalization conjured up to support the old power structure.

I suggested an experiment. I asked him if for the next week he would like to try sitting in my chair at the table and calling me "Shelly" rather than "Dad." I cold see the mixture of his excitement and anxiety at the prospect. Jon declined the invitation on the basis that he guessed that he had spent too many years in this sort of family to feel comfortable with such a radical change.

And so it went as he moved in and out of our lives for several weeks. Near the end of his stay he made certain to find me alone in the study one evening. He told me that it was important to him to talk with me about how each of us felt about the fact that I don't have very long to live.

It was a painful, powerful, loving exchange. He seemed comforted by some of the ways in which I have begun to come to peaceful terms with my dying and by my commitment to enjoying as I can what life I have left. For myself, I experienced him more clearly than ever as someone whom I love having as a son. And now I could see, too, that were I younger and not his father I would want him as my friend, and were he older and not my son, I would have been happy to have had a man such as he is becoming to have been my own father.

Soon after this talk, he went on his own way once more. A few days later I received a letter from him consisting simply of a salutation and a loving closing as the setting for a quoted story that he had come across. It was about a jazz musician whose piano playing we both enjoyed. The letter read:

Dear Dad,

"Relaxing between sets, Art Tatum sat at a table in a 52nd Street bistro, drinking beer from a bottle.

'But faith is your salvation,' said the brownskin girl.

And Art took a swig of his beer.

'Without it, you are lost,' said the brownskin girl, as blind Art Tatum sadly sipped his beer.

'All God's children are lost,' said Art, 'but only a few can play the piano.'"

Love,
Jon.

Chapter IV
Therapy as Theater

Often the miscast person who has developed a neurotic character style finds that his tragically heroic role brings on more needless suffering than satisfaction. When enduring more feelings of unhappiness than of being special becomes too burdensome, he may seek the help of a psychotherapist. Typically, he is *not* seeking to give up being a tragic figure. He simply would somehow like to work out a happy ending nonetheless. At my best as a therapist, I see myself as offering him an opportunity to give up his tragic script for a more playful, ad lib experience of spontaneity. For his part, he will not be willing to join me immediately in a life of improvised Theater of the Absurd. Instead first he will invite me to take part in his own tragic drama.

He himself has been successfully miscast. He has probably been playing his part of the neurotic longer and more consistently than I have been doing my thing of playing the part of the therapist. As a child, he was asked to pretend that he was some character other than himself. No doubt, his earliest reactions were attempts to resist the imposed role, but subtle rewards served to direct him into playing out his part. Finally, he has been subjected to an over-riding injunction which prohibited him from gaining any perspective, the compelling instruction to pretend that he is not pretending.

The theatrical magic of such a production creates its own reality. The power of pretending can move a theater audience to sympathy, anger, grief, and relief. If pretending can call forth such powerful responses in free agents who have merely stopped by for a few hours of entertainment, what they then may it evoke in someone who grows up trapped in such an illusory setting?

How does this paradoxical power of pretend work its magic? Let us consider an example which is neither the total immersion setting of the neurotic home situation on the one hand, nor the temporary voluntary theater audience visit on the other. It is one of those Kafkaesque social experiences which have the captive power of the former, in the seemingly free environment of the latter. Consider this report of an incident of pretending among the Zuni Indians of New Mexico. It was witnessed at the turn of the century by an anthropoligical field-worker:

A twelve-year-old girl was stricken with a nervous seizure directly after an adolescent boy had seized her hands. The youth was accused of sorcery and dragged before the court of the Bow priesthood. For an hour he denied having any knowledge of occult power, but this defense proved futile. Because the crime of sorcery was at that time still punished by death among the Zuni, the accused changed his tactics. He improvised a tale explaining the circumstances by which he had been initiated into sorcery. He said he had received two substances from his teachers, one which drove girls insane and another which cured them. This point constituted an ingenious precaution against later developments. Having been ordered to produce his medicines, he went home under guard and came back with two roots, which he proceeded to use in a complicated ritual. He simulated a trance after taking one of the drugs, and after taking the other he pretended to return to his normal state. Then he administered the remedy to the sick girl and declared her cured. The session was adjourned until the following day, but during the night the alleged sorcerer escaped. He was soon captured, and the girl's family set itself up as a court and continued the trial. Faced with the reluctance of his new judges to accept his first story, the boy then invented a new one. He told them that all his relatives and ancestors had been witches and that he had received marvelous powers from them. He claimed that he could assume the form of a cat, fill his mouth with cactus needles, and kill his victims—two infants, three girls, and two boys—by shooting the needles into them. These feats he claimed, were due to the magical powers of certain plumes which were used to change him and his family into shapes other than human. This last detail was a tactical error, for the judges called upon him to produce the plumes as proof of his new story. He gave various excuses which were rejected one after another, and he was forced to take his judges to his house. He began by declaring that the plumes were secreted in a wall that he could not destroy. He was commanded to go to work. After breaking down a section of wall and carefully examining the plaster, he tried to excuse himself by declaring that the plumes had been hidden two years before and that he could not remember their exact location. Forced to search again, he tried another wall, and after another hour's work, an old plume appeared in the plaster. He grabbed it eagerly and presented it to his persecutors as the magic device of which he had spoken. He was then made to explain the details of its use. Finally, dragged into the public plaza, he had to repeat his entire story (to which he added a wealth of new detail). He finished it with a pathetic speech in which he lamented the loss of supernatural power. Thus reassured, his listeners agreed to free him. [1]

In a sense the boy is challenged to create the role his judges have imposed. Paradoxically, he does so by his very attempts to save himself. His confession transforms the defendant into a witness for the prosecution. "With a mixture of cunning and good faith . . . (bit by bit he takes on) the impersonation which has been thrust upon him (until eventually, now pretending that he is no longer pretending, the hero has become) the dupe of his own impersonation."[2]

As if this were not complicated enough, when a neurotic victim of such miscasting seeks out a therapist to help him with his problems, he enters upon the stage of yet another theater. Here in my office, I too lead a life made up partially of illusions (as I do outside the office). Obviously becoming a therapist is not entirely a spontaneous act of good faith. Here too, pretending plays its part.

Again by way of illustration, I offer an anthropological field report. This time we will consider the description of the professional development of a shaman, the primitive society's equivalent of the psychotherapist.[3] The institutional training and credentials of our own culture are theatrical backdrops and props of the contemporary Western healer. They only cease seeming to be illusions to the extent that we have learned to pretend that they are *not* forms of pretending. All of this is no more than theater. Come look behind the scenes through this description of an autobiographical fragment of a Kwakiutl Indian from the Vancouver region of Canada:

> Quesalid (for this was the name he received when he became a sorcerer) did not believe in the powers of the sorcerers—or, more accurately, shamans, since this is a better term for their specific type of activity in certain regions of the world. Driven by curiosity about their tricks and by the desire to expose them, he began to associate with the shamans until one of them offered to make him a member of their group. Quesalid did not wait to be asked twice, and his narrative recounts the details of his first lessons, a curious mixture of pantomime, prestidigitation, and empirical knowledge, including the art of simulating fainting and nervous fits, the

learning of sacred songs, the technique for inducing vomiting, rather precise notions of auscultation and obstetrics, and the use of "dreamers," that is, spies who listen to private conversations and secretly convey to the shaman bits of information concerning the origins and symptoms of the ills suffered by different people. Above all, he learned the *ars magna* of one of the shamanistic schools of the Northwest Coast: The shaman hides a little tuft of down in a corner of his mouth, and he throws it up, covered with blood, at the proper moment—after having bitten his tongue or made his gum bleed—and solemnly presents it to his patient and the onlookers as the pathological foreign body extracted as a result of his sucking and manipulations.

His worst suspicions confirmed, Quesalid wanted to continue his inquiry. But he was no longer free. His apprenticeship among the shamans began to be noised about, and one day he was summoned by the family of a sick person who had dreamed of Quesalid as his healer. The first treatment (for which he received no payment, any more than he did for those which followed, since he had not completed the required four years of apprenticeship) was an outstanding success. Although Quesalid came to be known from that moment on as a "great shaman," he did not lose his critical faculties. He interpreted his success in psychological terms—it was successful "because he (the sick person) believed strongly in his dream about me." A more complex adventure made him in his own words, "hesitant and thinking about many things." Here he encountered several varieties of a "false supernatural," and was led to conclude that some forms were less false than others—those, of course, in which he had a personal stake and whose system he was, at the same time, surreptitiously building up in his mind. A summary of the adventure follows.

While visiting the neighboring Koskimo Indians, Quesalid attends a curing ceremony of his illustrious colleagues of the other tribe. To his great astonishment he observes a difference in their technique. Instead of spitting out the illness in the form of a "bloody worm" (the concealed down), the Koskimo shamans merely spit a little saliva into their hands, and they dare to claim that this is "the sickness." What is the value of this method? What is the theory behind it? In order to find out "the strength of the shamans, whether it was real or whether they only pretended to be shamans" like his fellow tribesmen, Quesalid requests and obtains permission to try his method in an instance where the Koskimo method has failed. The sick woman then declares herself cured . . .

Meanwhile, the Koskimo shamans, "ashamed" and discredited before their tribesmen, are also plunged into doubt. Their colleague has produced, the the form of a material object, the illness which they had always considered as spiritual in nature and had thus never dreamed of rendering visible. They send Quesalid an emissary to invite him to a secret meeting in a cave. Quesalid goes and his foreign colleagues expound their system to him: "Every sickness is a man: boils and swellings, and itch and scabs, and pimples and coughs and consumption and scrofula; and also this, stricture of the bladder and stomach aches . . . As soon as we get the soul of the sickness which is a man, then dies the sickness which is a man. Its body just disappears in our insides." If this theory is correct, what is there to show? And why, when Quesalid operates, does "the sickness stick to his hand?" But Quesalid takes refuge behind professional rules which forbid him to teach before completing four years of apprenticeship, and refuses to speak. He maintains his silence even when the Koskimo shamans send him their allegedly virgin daughters to try to seduce him and discover his secret.

Thereupon Quesalid returns to his village at Fort Rupert. He learns that the most reupted shaman of a neighboring clan, worried about Quesalid's growing renown, has challenged all his colleagues, inviting them to compete with him in curing several patients. Quesalid comes to the contest and observes the cures of his elder. Like the Koskimo, this shaman does not show the illness. He simply incorporates an invisible object, "what he called the sickness" into his headring, made of bark, or into his bird-shaped ritual rattle. These objects can hang suspended in mid-air, owing to the power of the illness which "bites" the house-posts or the shaman's hand. The usual drama unfolds. Quesalid is asked to intervene in cases judged hopeless by his predecessor, and he triumphs with his technique of the bloody worm.

Here we come to the truly pathetic part of the story. The old shaman, ashamed and despairing because of the ill-repute into which he has fallen and by the collapse of his therapeutic technique, sends his daughter to Quesalid to beg him for an interview, The latter finds his colleague sitting under a tree and the old shaman begins thus: "It won't be bad what we say to each other, friend, but only I wish you to try and save my life for me, so that I may not die of shame, for I am a plaything of our people on account of what you did last night. I pray you to have mercy and tell me what stuck on the palm of your hand last night. Was it the true sickness or was it only made up? For I beg you have mercy and tell me about the way you did it so that I can imitate you. Pity me, friend.

Silent at first, Quesalid begins by calling for explanations about the feats of the head-ring and the rattle. His colleague shows him the nail hidden in the head-ring which he can press at right angles into the post, and the way in which he tucks the head of his rattle between his finger joints to make it look as if the bird were hanging by its beak from his hand. He himself probably does nothing but lie and fake, simulating shamanism for material gain, for he admits to being "covetous for the property of the sick men." He knows that shamans cannot catch souls, "for . . . we all own a soul"; so he resorts to using tallow and pretends that "it is a soul . . . that white thing . . . sitting on my hand." The daughter then adds her entreaties to those of her father: "Do have mercy that he may live." But Quesalid remains silent. That very night, following this tragic conversation, the shaman disappears with his entire family, heartsick and feared by the community, who think that he may be tempted to take revenge. Needless fears: He returned a year later, but both he and his daughter had gone mad. Three years later, he died.

And Quesalid, rich in secrets, pursued his career, exposing the impostors and full of contempt for the profession. "Only one shaman was seen by me, who sucked at a sick man and I never found out whether he was a real shaman or only made up. Only for this reason I believe that he is a shaman; he does not allow those who are made well to pay him. I truly never once saw him laugh." Thus his original attitude has changed considerably. The radical negativism of the free thinker has given way to more moderate feelings. Real shamans do exist. And what about him? At the end of the narrative we cannot tell, but it is evident that he carries on his craft conscientiously, takes pride in his achievements, and warmly defends the technique of the bloody down against all rival schools. [4]

There is a saying among really talented psychotherapists: "There are no great therapists; there are only great patients." And yet, "Quesalid did not become a great shaman because he cured his patients; he cured his patients because he had become a great shaman.[5] Which os these contradictory statements is true?

I once knew an excellent hypno-therapist. Though some people are supposedly unhyponotizable he was reputed to be able to hypnotize anyone. I asked him how this could be so. He answered: "It's just the power of my reputation. If a patient comes to see me because he has heard what a great hypnotist I'm supposed to be, then it's practically guaranteed that as soon as he steps into my waiting-room, automatically he goes into a deep trance." And yet another expert in the field writes: "It takes an extremely good hypnotist to know who is hypnotizing whom."[6]

The nature of man's perception and understanding is in part determined by the unconscious forms which his imagination imposes on every experience. Whether or not I am at first aware of it, I will respond to the impact of the underlying structure of the patient's neurosis. Being with him on a continuing basis will immerse me in a psychological situation in which I will be in some ways transformed by the structure of his neurotic system. Like all such psychological structures, his neurosis operates in a self-regulating way to preserve its wholeness intact.

The patient, in turn, will be subjected to the impact of the underlying structure of a comparable social-psychological system. He will enter my system constituted by the created environment of my offering to be his therapist. *Neither of us can enter the other's situation without becoming a part of it.*

The patient enters my office, tragic scenario in hand. He does *not* simply mistake me for someone out of the past by recasting me as a parent out of his childhood (as implied by the Freudian psychoanalytic concept of transference). Rather I enter into his play (just as he enters into mine). For a time we each act out whatever part the other directs him to take.

Neither of us is to blame. That's just the way it has to be for a while. Gradually I become aware of the ways in which I am caught up in the patient's system. He and I join in the excitement of discovery. Together we become increasingly aware of the underlying structure in which we are embedded. If we manage to do this, then our mutual expanding consciousness shifts the scene. Our awareness allows the therapeutic system to subsume the neurotic system. This allows me to have more and more personal impact on his situation. In time this impact transforms the structure of his script. As a result, he increases his ability to improvise, and enlarges the repertoire of his life style.

If such a therapeutic transformation of the patient may eventually come about, first for a time I must be willing to risk being transformed by the patient. I too come to the situation with my own unresolved complexes, residuals of my own childhood miscastings. These alone would tempt me to act out a series of miscast roles with the patient. As Jung so poignantly admitted:

> For, twist and turn the matter as we may, the relations between doctor and patient remains a personal one within the impersonal framework of professional treatment. By no device can the treatment be anything but the product of mutual influence, in which the whole being of the doctor as well as that of his patient plays its part. In the treatment there is an encounter between two irrational factors, that is to say, between two persons who are not fixed and determinable quantities but who bring with them, besides their more or less clearly defined fields of consciousness, an indefinitely extended sphere of non-consciousness. [7]

Because of this projected counter-transference reaction I will at times miscast the patient into some role out of one of my own childhood scenarios. It is also certain that I will become engulfed in his transforming system. Both the conscious and unconscious miscasting which the patient brings to the therapy situation will affect me. My behavior at these times will be more in line with his psychological system than with my own.[8] As Levenson points out:

> In the therapy the therapist lives with the patient, knows what it's like to deal with him in its best and worst aspects, knows what he turns one into, what he calls out. This willingness to risk his own identity, to 'trip' with the patient, is the keystone of helpers from shamans to psychoanalysts. [9]

Earlier in my work beginning with each new patient would call forth my empty resolves. I would start out determined that *this* time, with *this* person, I will be truly objective This time I will *not* be manipulated. This time I will *not* participate in his craziness. But each time it was the same. There was no way for me to remain the detached expert, there was no way to be so completely separated by my professionalism that I could catch his act without joining the new patient in a duet. I always ended up playing the foil or becoming his dancing partner.

Not that I was consistently perceptive enough to recognize how I played out my role in every case. Many times the very way in which I did therapy served to mask the ways in which I was caught up in the patient's system. For example, I remember one young man who came to therapy complaining about a painful lack of confidence in his own judgment and a feeling that his way of seeing things was rarely accepted by others, particularly by people in authority. His father, he said, had always insisted that the patient didn't really know what he was talking about, and he was afraid that I would probably treat him with the same critical contempt for his point of view.

I understood his expectations about me to be a transference reaction. I responded pendantically with an interpretation. I told the patient that what was *really* going on was that he experienced the responses of people in authority *as though* they were treating him critically as his father had done. I understand now that my therpeutic intervention was an error. Instead of encouraging the patient to deal directly with the hazards inherent in our developing relationship I invited him to join me in playing a safe intellectual game. Cast as the good patient, he complied by obsessing unproductively with me for a while as I had requested. He had simply traded the script of his psuedo-reality for mine.

That time-wasting, risk-avoiding, stalling routine which we got into had a deadlier underlying structure. Neither of us was aware of it at the time. By interpreting the patient's behavior as I did, I was explaining his behavior to him. I was of course fulfilling the miscasting structure. I took the role of his contemptuous father. In effect, I had told him that *he* didn't really know what he was talking about, but that I did.[10]

At the time he had objected to my treating him the way his father did. I interpreted that "resistance" as well. In this way I directed him to pretend that I was not just pretending to be trying to help him. My interpretation demanded that he pretend that I knew the real from the unreal, and that he did not.

In recent years my work with patients has taken a different direction. I now recognize that there is no way *not* to get caught up in the structure of the patient's miscasting system. Instead I try to surrender willingly to that experience. Early in the work, I now tell each patient what he can expect. He will surely have all of the same kinds of problems in his relationship with me that he has had with other people whom he allowed to become important to him. I go on to promise that for a while I will get into all his madness with him (and some of my own). I assure him that we will get incredibly entangled in his numbers and routines (and sometimes in mine).

I assure the patient this is a hopeful complication. In these tangled performances lies the opportunity for us to experience together all that with which he struggles. In extricating ourselves from these entanglements lies the hope of finding ways to solve some of these problems. He must come to understand just how vulnerable I am to getting caught up in his life system. I go on to point out the patient will be well-advised to try to be as aware as he can be of what is going on. Often *I* will need *his* help if I am to be able to help him. He must watch what is happening between us.

It will be wise of him to point out how I am taking myself in. That way he can help me to unhook from any of his routines in which I begin to collaborate.

A new patient is often a bit wide-eyed and incredulous in response to this opening pitch of mine. He came to therapy expecting that as therapist, I would be saner than he believes himself to be. He assumed that I would be too strong to be taken in by his craziness. If I had posed as this perfect parent, we would have taken an alternate route. Most patients are prepared to invest several years of time and money in an attempt to make the impervious therapist vulnerable. They want to prove that he is at least as crazy as they are. Some of this wasted effort can be avoided by the therapist's revealing his own fallibility up front.

It takes a while for the patient to begin to accept that I am not one of the gods who can provide the divine machinery to bring about a happy ending for the unhappy drama of his life. It takes even longer for him to come to accept that I am not even a particularly heroic character. It is this recognition which threatens his discovering that we are both ordinary folk. It's hard to accept that there are no major or minor characters in life. This denouement sometimes takes a few years to come about.

One of the ways I bring this about is by admitting to whatever behavior or attitudes the patient accuses me of portraying. I let him know that he surely must be right in finding me critical, inattentive, over-protective, seductive, or the like. I do first ask that he consider for a moment what evidence he can find in his observations of my behavior that I *am* treating him the way he feels that I am. He may of course be projecting a distorting fantasy onto my innocently therapeutic blank screen. But more often than not, together we will find that we have unwittingly lived out the fantasy structure of his tragic life script.

Together the patient and I form a system. Each of us unwittingly tries to miscast the other into some role which will fit the dramatic structure which he brings to the therapeutic scene. The patient's way of seeing me is *not* a distortion. Being with him does for a time transform me. He may see me or describe me in ways that are somewhat exaggerated or symbolically caricatured to meet the heroic proportions of his tragic script. Nevertheless his neurotic "transference" perceptions of me are very real, and must be respected.

I will have participated in his transformingly dramatic life style. Only by admitting to my own participation can I increase our awareness in a way that will allow us to perform differently. This awareness allows us to begin to give up pretending that we are not pretending. We may be able to come to live with the heavy, but ultimately freeing metatheatrical consciousness, together we may be able to face a life in which there is no ultimate, higher or objective reality. For us there will be only each of our ordinary personal experiences of what is real. Its compelling impact will draw in the other. For a time I will participate in his personal drama, as he will become a part of mine.

Part II
The Play Opens

Chapter I
Theater Games

Though certain kinds of pretending may lead to neurotic character styles, pretending is by no means destructive in and of itself. Without some measure of pretending, how would we escape life's uncaring harshness, its impersonal buffeting, and its tedious sameness? Creative pretending as the form of fantasy and daydreaming affords pleasure, excitement, relief, and even hope. Pretending can provide a way of filling personal needs at times and in places in which we would otherwise have to do without. Each culture provides sanctioned ways of pretending which take people beyond the frustrations of everyday life. Such is the wonder of story-telling, the enthrallment of theater, and the grandeur of ceremony.

Pretending is the mining of the mother-lode of imagination. In fantasy we may find inspiration for new ways to live. In daydreaming we may rehearse future actions so that they can be approached with less fear and more grace. Reflection may even involve the practical planning which maps undeveloped projects by effectively solving problems in advance with a minimum of wasteful trial-and-error bungling.

Play is a special form of pretending. Life without play would be unbearably dreary. Being serious, realistic, and grown-up (whatever that all may mean) have their place and their own rewards. But all of this in the absence of play not only makes Jack a dull boy, but may make him a stuffy, pompous adult as well.

Some forms of play involved solitary musings, games of self against chance, or simply isolated secret bits of whimsy which have no impact on those around us. Other kinds of play require that at least one other person be involved. It is on this interpersonal play that I will be focusing in this chapter.

The communications involved in interpersonal play are by definition complex.[1] Almost all communications between people involve mood-signs or signals which amend or expand the denotative implications of words and gestures. So it is that the tone and stance which accompany a seemingly simple salutation of "Hey there!" determine whether we will hear it as neutral acknowledgment, word of welcome, or aggressive challenge.

Play requires a further elaboration, another level of abstraction which brings about the mutual understanding that "This is play!" In this meta-communication, the whole interaction is further commented upon so that I may know that when you called to me so aggressively, you were only horsing around, or that your very seductive tone was meant only to be flirtatious. If I misunderstand you by missing the meta-communication which would tell me that you are only playing, we may find ourselves in deep interpersonal troubles. Such misunderstandings lead to needless fights, and to sticky awkward interplays of embarrassment and hurt feelings.

Except in formal games such as sports and cardplaying the understanding that "This is play" is not made explicit and clearly agreed upon throughout by both parties. Even in tennis, or in bridge, when an opponent's aggressiveness becomes "too real," he may have to be admonished to "Remember, this is *only* a game!"

No matter how formalized or how subtly implicit, the expanded meaning of "This is play" always implies "these actions in which we now engage do not denote what those actions *for which they stand* would denote."[2] On the tennis court, "I'm going to kill you this time!" does not imply a threat of homicide, just as at the cocktail party, "You really turn me on!" does not *necessarily* imply a sexual invitation.

Interpersonal play can be great fun, or it can be highly destructive. It is safe and rewarding to play such games if we both know that we are only playing, if neither of us is forced to play against his will, and if neither insists on changing the rules without mutual consent. We may even play exploratory games such as conversation, sex, or therapy in which the purpose of the game is to discover the rules.

Life itself may be understood as such a search to discover rules which change merely because we become aware of them. Examples range widely. In science, the von Heisenberg uncertainty principle refers to the fact that the nature of energy and matter are found to be dependent on the way in which they are observed. Zen Buddhism teaches that there is nothing to learn, while Christianity instructs us that we may only have that which we are willing to surrender.

The contemporary drama which is made up almost exclusively of destructive interpersonal play is Edward Albee's "Who's Afraid of Virginia Woolf?"[3] The very title is a literary elaboration on a childhood game of pretend. Only now it is played by adults who pretend that they are too grown up to be afraid of the Big Bad Wolf.

Albee's painful comedy of bad manners takes place in the present, in a small New England college town, in the living room of a middle-aged faculty couple. Martha is the large, boisterous, aggressively needy college president's daughter married to George, the sterile, passive history professor who fails to live up to anyone's expectations, even his own. As George and Martha, they may be understood to represent a broad segment of marriage in America. They hate each other, but they need each other desperately.

Together they have attended a party given to welcome new faculty members. When they get home at two o'clock in the morning, George discovers that Martha has invited a new young couple over for a nightcap. Their guests are Nick, a good-looking new biology professor who turns out to be a shallow opportunist, and Honey, his mousey simpleton of a wife whom he has married for her money and under the pressure of her hysterical false pregnancy. The motif of reproductive creativity, real or illusory, is also played out in George and Martha's shared fantasy of a son who does not really exist.

These four spend the next three-and-a-half hours together, drinking until they gradually strip away all the illusions which mask their ugly unhappiness. They tease and threaten each other. They fight and screw, performing ineptly in both instances. Deceitfully, they trick one another, playing games without acknowledging that they do not mean what they say, forcing unwilling victims to participate in the destructive play, and changing the rules without warning. Their games include:

Humiliate the Host, Get the Guests, Hump the Hostess, Bring up the Baby, and Kill the Kid.

People do sometimes play destructive games with each other. Certainly this has become a popular way of describing neurotic interactions. We find such descriptions in the media. Participants in encounter groups are often "accused" of playing games, and some schools of psychotherapy depend on this as a central concept for defining personal unhappiness and its cure. The designation of certain behaviors as game-playing is always perjorative, usually moralistic, and often implies that the person could stop if only he made up his mind to do so and really tried hard. Some therapists seem to feel that whether one plays games or is "game-free" is life's only crucial issue.

The widespread use of the term "games" to describe the psychology of certain human relationships can be attributed to the impact of Eric Berne's best-seller, *Games People Play*.[4] This cleverly written little book was the popularization of the Berne anti-game-playing school of therapy, Transactional Analysis, more familiarly referred to as T.A. Berne's easy-to-remember, highly optimistic ideas have more recently been expanded and evangelized by psychiatrist Thomas A. Harris in his pop-psychological production, *I'm OK—You're OK*.[5] As a result, T.A. is now being practiced by thousands of therapists, and near-therapists throughout the Free World. T.A. training institutes have mushroomed faster than encounter group growth centers, institutes with truly American names, such as the Boston Congregational minister's school, "O.K. World, Inc."

What is the O.K. world of T.A. all about? It goes something like this.

If you're unhappy, the reason is that there is an unbalanced relationship among the three parts that make up every personality. These ego states are your Parent, your Adult, and your Child. Your Child ego is your source of fun and creativity. Your Adult is your rational self, sort of a computer. And your Parent is made up of behaviors copied from your parents or others in authority.

According to T.A., unless the mature Adult in you is plugged in, the too-superior, restrictive Parent or the inferiority-ridden, primitive Child will mess up most of your interpersonal transactions. The result will be chronically unhappy sequences of behavior, always involving an ulterior motive and an ultimately destructive payoff for the players. These behavior sequences are the games people play.

If you want to put your Adult back in charge, you have to learn the language of transactional analysis, the chalk-talk diagramming of the transactions, and most important you must learn the name of the game. The games T.A. has named include "Kick Me," "Uproar," "If It Weren't For Them," "Ain't It Awful," "Rape," and "Let's You and Him Fight."

The T.A. people use the term "life script" (within which these games are played) to describe "the blueprint for a life course."[6] They then schematically diagram the "switches" which the protagonist goes through in taking on one or another of the three main roles: Rescuer, Persecutor, or Victim. T.A. therapy is conducted in groups. In such a setting, the patient can be observed in action until the therapist and other group members can identify and analyze his transactions. Like the games, the life script is identified in some catchy way, such as by naming the patient's life-story, "Cinderella," "St. George and the Dragon," "King Midas," "The Lone Ranger," or some other well-known fairy-tale, myth, or pop-culture figure.

The T.A. labels are always outrageous simplifications of an unhappy life. "Exposure" of the patient's games and life-script is then used as a way of targeting him for the blame, the ridicule, and the exhortation of the group. If only he would see what he is up to, admit the error of his ways, and really try to live a life of positive adaptation with redeeming social meaning, then he would be able to say: "I'm O.K. and Everyone Else is O.K., Too."

This sort of triumphant evangelism is a mixture of Bill Graham and Norman Vincent Peale. The revival-tent group pressure to witness is overpowering. Preparation for the instant of conversion may take many months of T.A. group meetings, but the moment of illumination, combined with the resolve to break out of the sinful life, is always a peak experience. Its effects last about as long as the impact of the Encounter Group "Esalen-all-purpose-cop-out-hug."

Like New Year's Resolutions, the T.A. life-script conversions dissipate quickly unless the patient remains dependent on a doctrinaire, inspirationally supportive group. If a patient comes to live the T.A. life of adaptation to that particularly reassuring closed system, then his life style is descibed as "autonomy." It reminds me of a friend's comment after having visited and researched many of the Synanon-type, communally-authoritarian, residential centers for the treatment of heroin addiction. He said wryly, "Personally, I'd rather be a junkie!"

In Transactional Analysis, Berne (much like Janov, the founder of Primal or Tantrum Therapy), sees neurotic patterns or scripts as being based on consciously will decisions. He seems unable to acknowledge that sometimes people are helpless to change their self-destructive or socially noxious ways of behaving. But success is *not* the significant measure of whether or not someone is trying his best. It is *not* true, that if only we tried hard enough, we could do what is right, or at least what we say we wish to do.

A patient comes to therapy, trying to change. But some things simply cannot be accomplished until a person has had enough help and feels safe enough to be ready to change. He may well be trying as hard as he can, and still not be able to break free. Bad enough to be stuck in such a frustrating struggle without being further burdened by the therapist's accusation that he is simply playing a game, that if he is not changing it's because he doesn't want to. Psychotherapy patients are often too hard on themselves already, blaming themselves for doing things they cannot help, for not venturing into new areas which are too terrifying to yet be entered.

Some wounds never fully heal. A person can have been treated badly too often, for too long, and without enough sustaining good experiences, so that he may always have to walk this life with an emotional limp. Berne seems without respect for people's struggles with some problems which may never be fully soluble.

At times, his superficial, self-righteous demands on people, his smart-ass ridiculing acronyms, his simplistic diagrams, are simply unkind. Centuries of struggle not only for survival and gain, but for spiritual, poetic, and ethical goals as well, are reduced to tricky manipulations to seek reward and to avoid punishment. It is as if man lived outside of the cry of history and the ambiguity of inevitable uncertainty, guilt, and anxiety. T.A. is terribly reassuring, offers clever micro-help, but finally boils down to a reductive contemptuous view of human beings, the wisdom of which is limited and costly.

T.A. sacrifices some of what is most touching and compelling in the insolubly human condition to that which is most practical and effective in the promising idea of progress. There is nothing really to cry about. Weeping is seen as no more than noisy manipulative display. Berne does not detail his case for the emptiness of tears. For the moment he is best answered by citing Unamuno's fine anecdote about Solon, one of the Seven Sages of Athens:

> *"Why do you weep for the death of your son," the*
> *skeptic asked Solon, "when it avails nothing?"*
> *"I weep," replied Solon, "precisely because it*
> *avails nothing."*[7]

Weeping is not the only fundamental human expressive function that Berne discredits. For all of his stated emphasis on game-free spontaneity, he disparages the expression of anger as mostly no more than a "racket" designed to achieve some concealed and unworthy end. "What good does it do to get angry?" he asks when "It seldom accomplishes anything that cannot be done better without it."[8]

Not only does he deny that anger is a biological necessity, a natural aspect of the man/beast, but further, in his good old American know-how pragmatic orientation, he is concerned only with a kind of manipulative accomplishment.

I certainly agree that anger is not *always* politically expedient. When I can help it, I never shout at policemen, or at other adversaries who are armed and dangerous. And what's more, I know that my own open show of anger may well not change the other in some situations.

Yet it is crucial, first, that I know *when* I feel angry. Next, it is helpful for me to be able to decide if my anger is *authentic*, by distinguishing it from that defensive pseudo-aggression which rises up to disguise my helplessness or hurt. Still, there remain two important functions of my expressed anger. My authentic anger arises when others hurt me needlessly. I cannot always get people to treat me well (or at least not hurt me) on the basis of their loving and respecting me. Yet I must survive intact if I can. And so, when someone who does not care how I feel treats me badly, I always try to make it expensive for him, by being as unpleasantly angry as is needed in response. If he will not stop treating me badly out of concern for me, then let him do so out of fear of my retaliation.

And second, though by no means less important, the expression of my anger is a way of dealing with my own inner space, as well as a way of transacting with others in my external surroundings. So it is, that often I rage simply to restore my own inner calm, without any expectation that I will be truly heard and responded to. I find that it is good for my digestion, and it sure beats being depressed.

All of this has nothing to do with Berne's model for the injustice-collector's game of "Now I've Got You, You Son of a Bitch" (NIGYSOBO). Certainly, the neurotic behavior pattern described in such a game is a masochistic seeking of conflict. For people who play this game, the expression of anger is a temporary and destructive tension-reducer which neither improves relationships with other people nor frees the compulsive collector of injustices from his own painfully old, and unrecognized bitterness.

In dealing with the delayed or unrecognized resentment in the patient who only discovers that he is angry once he is safely out of the anger-provoking situation, Berne is typically glib and simplistic. Aphoristically, he dispenses with this frequent neurotic distress as follows: "The rule for staircase anger is . . . 'If you didn't say it on the spot, don't go back to say it afterward as you intuition was probably right in the first place.' The best policy is to wait until the next occasion, and then if you are really ready to do better, you will."

In my experience, this sort of homely philosophy simply obscures the patient's options, and delays his movement toward becoming aware of his anger when it actually arises. If, instead, the patient is helped to see that he does not have to get it right *before* he can get it right, he can be helped to start where he is and to become more of the sort of person he would like to be. That is, he may be angered by how someone treats him, but because of earlier assaults on his right to express anger, be put off from becoming aware of his resentment until he is a safe distance from the offending party.

He need only realize that he then has the option of going back upstairs, or of calling his attacker on the phone, or writing him a letter. If this feels right to him, he will be free to express his anger by having bypassed the neurotic defenses which kept him unaware of his anger on the spot. This leaves him free to deal openly with the other, and put himself in touch with his hidden anxieties. If the defensive delay is bracketed in this way it will gradually drop out. The time gap between the arousal of anger and his awareness of it will be closed by the inevitability of his open expression of feelings. Eventually he can reach the point where he knows what he feels, when he feels it, and is free to decide if and how to let it out.

Ironically then, therapy may begin with trick against trick. The therapist as trickster/healer[9] introduces the *game of therapy* in order to create disinterest in the *game of neurosis*. Yet I do *not* mean to imply that the patient must lose in order for the therapist to win. My goal as therapist does not have to do with changing the patient. Change is *his* goal. My purpose is to carry out the work impeccably without regard for the results.[10] Some days I do brilliantly creative work and the patients seems to get nowhere. Other days, because I am tired, troubled, or irresponsible, I do mediocre or poor work and in response to my half-assed performance the patient is transformed, achieving new ways to happiness beyond his impatient hopes. On which days should I be satisfied, on his good days or on my own?

My use of games is merely stage magic which may distract the patient from his everyday sham. It is no more than an invitation to creative play which offers the patient the opportunity to be freed for the moment from his chronically destructive neurotic games. It is a bit like sidewalk puppetshows in a ghetto. In itself, such theater solves no problems. Yet a delinquent kid may become engaged in a way which promises to free his imagination so that he will be better able to solve his "real" problems.

The strategy of trick against trick is an old one. It is the "hair of the dog that bit you" and the thief you set "to catch a thief." In Tantric Yoga, it is the indulgence in passion which frees a man from passion. It is that:

A man who is poisoned may be cured by another poison, the antidote. Water in the air is removed by more water, a thorn in the skin by another thorn. So wise men rid themselves of passion by yet more passion. As a washerman uses dirt to wash clean a garment, so, with impurity, the wise man makes himself pure.[11]

The therapist's theater games are many. They include his encouraging expectations that the entire therapeutic stage set is a mysterious power place in which wonderous things can happen. Like previous hits, a long run, and good reviews, the therapist's training and reputation excite hope in the patient.

His stage directions range from the simple supportively instructive suggestion that the patient's problems are familiar and soluble, to elaborate therapeutic strategies which put the patient into a double-bind from which his only escape is into mental health.[12] An example of the latter more elegant ledgerdemain would be the trick of dealing with a problem of frequent uncontrollable arguments between a married couple.

The therapist tells them that he wants them to have several fights before the three meet again. If they are to be in therapy with him they must pay careful attention to every fight they have during the following week. They must each take notes on the sequence as it happens so that they can present the problem for solution next session. If they follow the instructions to fight, they are already yielding to the therapist's control. If they pay attention and take notes, they will be fighting but no longer in an uncontrolled way. If they choose not to fight (in order to resist the therapist's intervention) they will have made him successful in solving their presenting problems.

Some of the therapist's games depend on theatrical props which facilitate the patient's tricking himself into feeling how he would like to feel or doing what he would like to do. One example is the Kleenex box that lets the patient give himself permission to cry during his visits to the therapist. Its obviously unobtrusive placement is beside the patient's chair. It is best if there is none beside the therapist's chair.

The analyst's couch is compellingly effective in convincing patients that they can reclaim childhood memories, associate freely, and gain more ready access to their dreams and fantasies. My own office is usually hauntingly darkened and its walls are hung with primitive, mythic, and surrealistic images. Try being hard-headedly "realistic" and self-controlled in an atmosphere like that!

Still there must be different strokes for different folks. Stock properties won't always do. Sometimes new games must be invented, new props improvised. One patient had difficulty asserting herself. It was hard for her not to give in when other people demanded that she go along with their wishes rather than her own. Until her anxiety had been diminished sufficiently for her to be able to fend better for herself, I invited her to play a game with me that might help. I gave her a signed letter on my professional stationery, a "doctor's note" excusing her from submitting to other people's demands on the grounds that it would be injurious to her mental health. It worked as well as any note I ever wrote to get one of my kids temporarily excused from a physical education class.

My "game" with Ellen was more spontaneous and genuine, less hokey, but ultimately just as theatrical (in the best sense).

I had liked Ellen from the first time that I met her. She had come to my office seeking psychotherapy, wanting help with her unhappy underestimation of herself. Nothing she did was sufficient to make her confident, and no amount of apparent affection from others could make her feel she was lovable. My liking for her was no more to be trusted than anyone else's. It was perhaps even more suspect because of her projected overestimation of my importance.

Nonetheless, the work went well. Ellen gradually revealed herself and got to know me better. She expressed forbidden feelings, found hidden strengths, and reorganized the priorities in her life. All in all, she not only did better, but began to feel increasingly better about who she was. Still at this point she found it hard to simply feel good from inside, to recognize herself as a decent and lovable human being, no longer the child of uncertain worth on consignment to an approval-withholding family.

During this second act Ellen had a very powerful set of new experiences. Through these for the first time she acquired a clear sense that she was *not* responsible for many of the awful things that had occurred in her life. It was very moving for me to be with her as she came to this unburdening piece of understanding. I felt closer to Ellen and was happy for her, and I was also much encouraged by her inspiring emancipation and encouraging comradeship along the way of my often overburdened world-weary trek from out of the morass of my own family scene.

At the time I had just completed Part I of this book. It was my first excursion into writing about my childhood with all of its pain, with some pathos, and hopefully with some liberating humor. I felt very vulnerable and uncertain about how effective this new sort of writing would be. It seemed suddenly just right to tell Ellen about the manuscript and to expose my uneasiness about its worth to her. I offered to let her read it if she wanted to, on the condition that she would not show it to anyone else.

Feeling chosen, she was very responsive. She took it home and read it with great interest. The next time I saw her, she told me how painfully compelling she found my account of my own childhood struggle. She understood more clearly than ever how it is that she and I felt so close to one another. but she could not make sense of why I should trust *her* with something so precious and fragile. It did make her feel worthwhile and she talked of wishing she had a safe in which to put it when she got home. It was· precious and for the moment she felt that she was too. It had been a marvelous week for her as she dealt with other people with increased ease and confidence. Yet her sense of increased self-worth obviously depended very much on the magic of having been given this splendid ritual treasure.

It was then that I told her the story of the Medieval knight who attended a course at the local dragon-slaying school. Several other young knights also attended this special class taught by Merlin, the magician.

Our anti-hero went to Merlin the first day to let him know that he would probably not do well in the course because he was a coward and was sure he would be much too frightened and inept ever to be able to slay a dragon. Merlin said he need not worry because there was a magic dragon-slaying sword which he would give the cowardly young knight. With such a sword in hand there was no way that anyone could fail in slaying any dragon. The knight was delighted to have this official magic prop with which any knight, no matter how worthless, could kill a dragon. From the first field trip on, magic sword in hand, the cowardly knight slew dragon after dragon, freeing one maiden after another.

One day toward the end of the term, Merlin sprung a pop quiz on the class which the young knight was attending. The students were to go out in the field and kill a dragon that very day. In the flurry of excitement as all the young knights rushed off to prove their mettle, our anti-hero grabbed the wrong sword from the rack. Soon he found himself at the mouth of a cave from which he was to free a bound maiden. Her fire-breathing captor came rushing out. Not knowing that he had picked the wrong weapon, the young knight drew back his sword in preparation for undoing the charging dragon. As he was about to strike, he noticed that he had taken the wrong sword. No magic sword this, just your ordinary adequate-for-good-knights-only sword.

It was too late to stop. He brought down the ordinary sword with a trained sweep of his arm, and to his surprise and delight, off came the head of still another dragon.

Returning to the class, dragon's head tied to his belt, sword in hand, and maiden in tow, he rushed to tell Merlin of his mistake and of his unexplainable recovery.

Merlin laughed when he heard the young knight's story. His answer to the young knight was: "I thought that you would have guessed by now. None of the swords are magic and none of them ever have been. The only magic is in believing."

Patients sometimes misunderstand the game as one in which they can believe in themselves only because I believe in them. This is a useful mistake for them to make. It gives me the power they need at a time when they mistakenly think that I am more reliable than they are. My own understanding of the game is one in which I let the patient believe in me until he is ready to believe in himself.

The therapist must help the patient to fool himself for a while, but he himself must recognize that his engaging the patient's faith is no more than creative play, a good game, imaginative theater. Woe-betide the therapist who begins to feel that he is somehow more human than the patient, more powerful, or something special! We all know the pathetic foolishness of the therapist who mistakes the patient's reaction for a realistic appraisal of his own worth. There are little old psychoanalysts, some of whom are bald, short, and fat, dull straight-arrows who think of themselves as excitingly dynamic and irresistably sexy because every twenty year old lovely who enters their office seeking therapy falls in love with them. These comic figures are only the obvious examples of the potential corruption to anyone who would risk a career that attracts the discipleship of temporary groupies.

Rama Krishna tells this story to warn therapists and other gurus never to take themselves too seriously:

> Tapobana, the Master, had a disciple who served him with irreproachable diligence. It was solely because of this diligence and the services he rendered that Tapobana kept him, for he found the disciple rather stupid.
>
> One day, the rumor spread throughout the whole region that Tapobana's disciple had walked on water; that he had been seen crossing the river as one crosses the street.
>
> Tapobana called his disciple and questioned him.
>
> "Is what people are saying about you possible? Is it really true that you crossed the river walking on the water?"

"What could be more natural?" answered his follower. "It is thanks to you, Blessed One, that I walked on water. At every step I repeated your saintly name and that is what upheld me."

And Tapobana thought to himself, "If the disciple can walk on water, what can the Master not do? If it is in my name that the miracle takes place, I must possess power I did not suspect and holiness of which I have not been sufficiently aware. After all, I have never tried to cross the river as if I were crossing the street."

And without more ado, he ran to the river bank. Without hesitation, he set his foot on the water, and with unshakable faith repeated, "Me, me, me . . . " And sank. [1][3]

As a psychotherapist, and teacher of psychotherapy, I too surround myself with disciples, complain about their demands, and corrupt myself on their applause and adoration. But our relationship is as dangerously misleading to them as it is to me. To the extent that any of us become so immersed in the theatrical aspects of our coming together that he lose sight of the needed irreverence, he makes a big mistake. I am reminded of a story about an Indian Holy Man and his disciples:

He would sit for hours alone in his cave meditating, his only companion being a favourite cat which he tied to a post in his cave during his periods of meditation. As years went by his fame spread and he soon had a number of pupils who came to learn from him and who made him their guru or teacher. He instructed his pupils to meditate as he did. Soon each pupil could be observed meditating with a cat tied to a post by his side. [1][4]

Chapter II
Taking Your Own Part

What is a man to do when he must decide between the loneliness of independence and the self-sacrifice of conformity? There are times when the only options which seem available are for a man to suffer the seemingly unbearable isolation and ambiguity of preserving his integrity by standing alone, to savor the sweet comfort of certainty and surrender which come with becoming a part of the herd. No one is beyond such temptations.

Even Solzhenitsyn, that consummate rebel, that testimonial to what hardship a man may bear and still remain true to his individualism of spirit, even he has seen the options, and has been tempted. And so even after half-a-lifetime of political imprisonment in the Siberian wastelands, Aleksander Solzhenitsyn can still write of the seductive pull of conformity:

> I remember very well that right after officer candidate school I experienced the *happiness of simplification,* of being a military man and *not having to think things through;* the *happiness of* being immersed in the life *everyone else lived,* that was *accepted* in our military milieu; the happiness of forgetting some of the spiritual subtleties inculcated since childhood. [1]

As he looked back on himself and others, on those who had stood fast as opposed to those who had sold out, he could not give in to some simple sifting into good guys and bad buys. He remains both graced and burdened by his continuing recognition that people choose differing courses of action, not because some are good and others evil, but because they understand the options differently one man from another:

> To do evil a human being must first of all believe that what he's doing is good, or else that it's a well-considered act in conformity with natural law.

Fortunately, it is in the nature of the human being to seek a *justification* for his actions. [2]

This issue of how a man may view his options when faced with the dilemma of either standing alone or joining the crowd is the central theme of Eugene Ionesco's play *Rhinoceros*.[3] Like most of the other plays which I will be discussing in this section of the book, *Rhinoceros* is a clear instance of the Theater of the Absurd.

In ancient Greek tragedy, and much of the drama which followed it:

> . . . *the ultimate realities concerned were generally known and universally accepted metaphysical systems* . . .

The Theater of the Absurd is one aspect of contemporary metatheater. As such, it:

> . . . expresses the absence of any such generally accepted cosmic system of values. Hence, much more modestly, the Theater of the Absurd makes no pretence at explaining the ways of God to man. It can merely present, in anxiety or with derision, an individual human being's intuition of the ultimate realities as he experiences them; the fruits of one man's descent into the depths of his personality, his dreams, fantasies, and nightmares. [4]

The Theater of the Absurd is no longer a storytelling theater of events in sequence, but rather a theater of situations. Let us beware of finding in these plays some moral or social reference. We would be better served by them if we could simply let them deepen our sense of the ridiculous existential situation which makes up each man's unreasonable life.

Ionesco's *Rhinoceros* takes place in a small peaceful European town. The quiet lives of its inhabitants are suddenly disrupted by the appearance of a rhinoceros, trampling through the streets. Soon more beasts appear. After the first comes another, then three, then four, their number increasing until the transformation develops into a "movement," which threatens to become universal.

Each person in the town responds in his own characteristic style to seeing men change into beasts without warning or explanation. The logician approaches the situation with an air of detached rationality. The Marxist wants to know what its impact will be on the working class. The last words of the Entrepreneur are "We must move with the times!" The man who fears isolation, who wants to be part of "the great universal family," can retain no more independence than is expressed in the rationalization" . . . if you're going to criticize, it's better to do so from the inside."

How are we to understand these physiological transformations of men into beasts? Are they merely metaphors of social change, symbolic expressions of psychological disease, or are they contemporary fables containing morals to be learned? Ionesco himself grew up during the rise of Fascism in Rumania. Surely in one sense the rhinoceroses are Nazis.

Yet even Fascism is only a human event. Human beings are forever trapped in a world without ultimate meanings. Political movements may be no more than a desperate grab for something worth doing, worth being a part of, worth hoping for.

In Ionesco's strange play, the pull of the trampling herd leads one character after another to succumb to the excitement of becoming a part of what everyone else is doing. In the final scene, only Berenger, the anti-hero and his girlfriend Daisy remain.

Now, Berenger must face even the loss of his sweet, reasonable, accommodatingly sensible Daisy. As she approaches the threshold of transformation into what had been a beast she feared and could not stand, she begins to explain:

> Where is your imagination? There are many sides to reality. Choose the one that's best for you. Escape into the world of the imagination . . . [5]

> We must adapt ourselves and try and get on with them . . . [6]

> There is no such thing as absolute right. It's the world that's right—not you and me . . . [7]

Berenger is unable to convince her to stay. He takes his stand nonetheless in near-heroic terms, vowing:

Well, in spite of everything, I swear to you I'll never give in, never! [8]

In earlier plays we would be left with Berenger at the barricades. Overcoming human frailty out of a commitment to higher principle, he would be headed for catastrophe that would make better men of us all. But not in the Theater of the Absurd. Here he turns out to be no more than a frightened hero-in-spite-of-himself.

His curtain speech reveals everyman's existential situation. Each of us can be no more than ourselves. To glorify *doing what we have to do* into some sort of mock-heroics is more than absurd. It's ridiculous! Listen to Berenger and see if you can hear *yourself.* Finally he is all alone. He is the last man. He says:

> Now I'm all on my own . . . But they won't get me. . . . You won't get me!. . . I'm not joining you; I don't understand you! I'm staying as I am. I'm a human being. A human being . . . [9]
>
> [As he examines his face, the previously ugly rhinoceros heads begin to seem more attractive than his own isolated human ugliness.] I'm not good-looking, I'm not good-looking . . .They're the good-looking ones. I was wrong! Oh, how I wish I was like them! I haven't got any horns, more's the pity! A smooth brow looks so ugly. I need one or two horns to give my sagging face a lift. Perhaps one will grow and I needn't be ashamed any more—then I could go on and join them. But it will never grow! . . . My hands are so limp—oh, why won't they get rough! . . . My skin is so slack. I can't stand this white hairy body. Oh I'd love to have a hard skin in that wonderful dull green colour— a skin that looks decent naked without any hair on it, like theirs! . . . Their song is charming—a bit rugged perhaps, but it does have charm! I wish I could do it! [He tries to imitate them] Ahh, ahh, brr! No . . . [he cannot].
>
> Now I'm a monster, just a monster. Now I'll never become a rhinoceros, never, never! . . . I'm so ugly! People who try to hang on to their individuality always come to a bad end! [10]

At this point it is clear that Berenger has no choice. He can't become a rhinoceros even though he wants to. Watch for the uneasy image of himself as he snaps out of his despair. His final words are:

Ah well, too bad! I'll take on the whole of them! I'll put up a fight against the lot of them, the whole lot of them! I'm the last man left, and I'm staying that way until the end. I'm not capitulating!

CURTAIN[11]

How well I know the temptation to play the martyred hero when I am in fact doing no more than I must. As an introvert, for better or for worse, I derive most of the meaning in my own life from the inner world of my own experience, rather than from the outer world of activities and other people. Often enough I stand over against group pressures simply because it's easier than going along. I feel embarrassed to recall how many times I accepted the undeserved admiration of others who saw my personal stands as heroic personal sacrifices of approval and community.

For the most part, approval from other people seems irrelevant and immersion in community feels suffocatingly uncomfortable. I am no noble man-of-principle who would sacrifice the world for the preservation of his honor. I am merely a peculiar and determined character so completely enchanted with the inner space of my mind that I do not even notice what others think of me. That's part of the reason why it is so easy for me to do psychotherapy in an atmosphere that is largely free of social conventions.

I have written elsewhere of my efforts to conduct the work of psychotherapy in the absence of deferential social ceremonial gestures.[12] Without such rituals, people move more quickly into the underlying primitive urges which so often go unrecognized in the mannered running of our lives. Unbuffered by the social lubrication of such civilized gloss, intimacy between people is more easily and immediately established.

I recently became aware of the meaning of an unrecognized residue of such ceremonial behavior in my own work as a group psychotherapist. The therapy groups I run are open-ended. As some patients finish their work in groups they leave and others are brought in to take their places. The only constant is the co-leadership of the group. At some point, my cotherapist and I may find ourselves running a group in which none of the original members are any longer present. It is as though we were the parents of a family. The children have absolutely crucial experiences with us while they are still at home but they are just passing through.

For a long while, it has been my practice not to bother with social introductions when bringing in a new patient. It had seemed to me that if I introduced the patients to one another, it would be a way of taking care of them. By creating an air of pseudo-mutality, I would simply be putting off the work of their dealing with their real feelings. When a new member enters the group, there is no way that he can completely escape feeling both frightened and resentful at being an outsider. The group may look forward to the coming of a new member. Yet surely they will resent his presence there as a threatening intruder. In non-therapeutic social situations, it is customary to make formal introductions at such points. These gestures inhibit the dangerous hostilities between the already established social group and the "visitor."

I have long been clear enough about all this to be comfortable in *not* introducing a new patient to the group. Nonetheless, I had somehow continued to introduce each new patient to my co-therapist. Recently, a new patient entered the group. A couple of weeks later a number of patients began to complain about my not taking good enough care of them. They felt that I could make things much easier if I took the trouble to introduce the people. Some even wanted me to let them know in advance when a new patient would be coming into the group. Perhaps I might even give them a chance to decide about whether or not a new patient would be accepted. I was open in my expression of amusement at the notion that I would take care of them in this way. All they were asking was that I surrender my right to make these choices while still being stuck with the responsibility of being the therapist in the group.

Then somebody made a mistake. One of the patients: "Well, if you won't introduce new patients to any of us, how come you introduce them to Jane (the co-therapist)?"

I thought a moment. Then I suddenly understood. I

answered: "Thank you, that was very helpful. I can see now that I have for years introduced new patients to Jane, because I count on her even after the rest of you leave. It's like deferring to a mate, like Poppa giving a special appeasement to Momma because once the kids are gone they'll have no one but each other."

The group made it clear that this was not the answer they had expected. Encouraged by this, I went one: "Now that it's clear to me, I promise that from now on I won't introduce new patients to anyone. I'll just take my chances on getting along with Jane. If we can't get along after the kids have gone, I guess we'll just have to get a divorce."

Two weeks later another new patient was brought into the group. This kicked off a great deal of the unfinished business of the patients' resenting my unwillingness to take care of them. It was heightened by the fact that the new patient had come in late. He did not even have a chance to introduce himself in the waiting room before the group session.

This time the co-therapist and I dealt with the objection by simply reflecting that of course the patients were still resentful at our not having things made easier for them. We acknowledged that this violated their social expectations about how people ought to be treated when newcomers enter the group. Still we stood firm without justifying ourselves. Neither trying to push our opinions onto the patients, nor discrediting how they felt about all of this, we did try to learn something from the altercation by exploring and interpreting the extra hidden meanings which lay beneath some of the protestations.

One of the patients complained that the new members were coming in too quickly and that she's hardly gotten used to one when the next one was there. This was used as an opportunity to explore her feelings about how difficult it was for her as her younger brothers were born, one seemingly right after the other. She had never gotten some of the needed little girl space for herself.

One man had grown up in an atmosphere charged with punishment whenever he outshined his brother. He was afraid the presence of the new patient would inhibit his own freedom to seek the group's attention.

Another patient said that this business of bringing in new patients would be okay except for the fact that we did not prepare group members for their coming. This was explored in terms of whether or not the patient had been prepared for the coming of younger sibs when she was little. The validity of this therapeutic intervention was confirmed by her coming up with a previously unshared memory. She told of an argument on the playground with another child in which she had insisted that pregnancy did not last nine months but only four. It turned out that her misconception had occurred because her parents did not tell her about the forthcoming sibling until the mother was five months pregnant.

We went on with the interpretive work we were into, walking the walk and talking the talk of analytic psychotherapists. I found I was doing a bit of gratuitious expounding. I explained my theory that preparation for a new patient coming does not help the group, that in fact it makes it harder for older members to show their anger.

Suddenly it dawned on me. For years I had been an only child. When I was thirteen, my mother became pregnant. I was prepared, and prepared, and prepared. Every day I was told that a wonderful baby sister would be coming, that I would love her very much, that I would enjoy taking care of her. I was even to have the privilege of giving up my room for her when she came. It was no wonder that preparation for the coming of an intruder seemed to me to be an untrustworthy and oppressive inhibitor of anger among those already present.

I told the group about my experience as a kid and of my insight of that moment. Unconsciously, this unexplored childhood experience of my own had determined a seemingly carefully thought out logistical approach to this aspect of group psychotherapy.

The identified patients were supportively appreciative of our common human frailty. They always are. I felt accepted and closer to them once more. Now my only problem is, what the hell am I to do from now on about the question of introducing new patients into the group?

Jane and I and the other group patients can now see that what had seemed like a carefully considered option on my part was no more than an unconsciously over-determined, compulsively repeated struggle with the past. Once this piece of my childhood is worked through, I will no longer have to repeat my defense against it. But how am I ever to know what is real, and freely chosen, and here and now? So much of what I do is what I must do, and yet so often it all seems so right, so real, so reasonable.

For some people, checking on what other people think is a help. The consensual validation of seeing things as others see them, is reality enough for some. But alas, and hooray, it's not enough for me. As a kid, I often did not fit in. My folks told me: "The whole world can't be crazy and you sane!" For a while, I thought they must be right, I must be crazy. But later I decided that they were wrong, that sometimes the whole world was crazy, and only I was sane. When I am able to retain the broadest perspective, I realize that *comparison is no way to judge what is real.* But when I am most into my introvertedly intuitive self, then I know that Shaw was clearly right when he pointed out that "Fifty million Frenchmen can't be right."[13]

Sorting out when we have live options and when we do not is often difficult. Without the possibility of being certain of our assessments we must learn to do the best we can and to find it sufficient. And when we have done all that we can we must learn to give up and to forgive ourselves for not having been able to do more. The therapist throws his weight where it is needed in this state of imbalance. The self-indulgent patients who would give up before they have to, he confronts with their responsibilities to themselves. But those who are too hard on themselves, he supportively accepts as having already tried to do more than they could.

The options of lonely independence versus self-sacrificing conformity are only one of the polarities each person must face. Life is often hard, and there are times when each person feels unprepared for what he must do. Everyone has moments when he feels too weak, too weary, too little to live his overwhelming life completely on his own.

There are many options, but one alone is fundamental. Camus tells us that

> There is but one truly serious philosophical problem, and that is suicide. Judging whether life is or is not worth living amounts to answering the fundamental question of philosophy. All the rest . . . comes afterwards. (All the rest) . . . are games.[14]

I am no emotional virgin to the romance of suicide. I have written elsewhere of my personal struggle over whether or not to end my own life.[15] A few of my relatives, some of my friends, and many of my patients have talked with me of their feeling like killing themselves. One member of each group has done so. An aunt hurled herself and her despair from the roof-ledge of a New York tenement. A strange sad friend intentionally over-dosed with a massive injection of heroin with which he had for several years tried to fix his pain. A psychotherapy patient left his sleeping-pill filled corpse on the living room floor of his vacationing parents' apartment, a vengeful reminder of the many ways he felt that they had ruined the few pleasures of his own short and unhappy life.

I believe that each person has a right to exercise this option of taking his own life. I feel a strong and compassionate tie to people who are going through the anguish and the hopelessness which makes them feel like committing suicide. But when someone I know *does* kill himself, I react with anger born of helplessness and with bitter amusement born of the senselessness of it all. I know of no way to resolve this inconsistency in myself. For the most part, it feels like an acceptable part of my unreasonableness.

If one of my patients is seriously considering suicide, I urge only that he delay long enough to be very clear as to what this decision is all about. Dying, like living, should be met with personal clarity and commitment.

Recently, within a period of a few weeks, I had the opportunity to attempt two innovative interventions in the supervision of therapists who were treating suicidal patients. Each intervention was a scary, exciting, and in its own way a surprisingly rewarding experience.

In each case the patient was present. I do supervision in this way for two reasons. The patient must be treated with the respect warranted by another human being (rather than a case to be gossiped about). And too, if the patient were not present, how then could I work my theater magic on this central character?

I offer the two vignettes merely as tales to be told without theoretical explanation or critical comment. In each instance my focus will be on how the patient experienced the supervisory presence and its consequent impact on his or her suicidal option.

The first of my suicidal supervisory interventions required redistributing responsibility. Several months earlier, Dr. R. had brought a young man to my supervisory seminar. The focused concern of both the therapist and the patient was the latter's repeated suicidal "gestures" (non-lethal over-doses of tranquilizers). My supervisory work with the couple primarily involved taking the patient's suicidal behavior seriously. I encouraged the therapist to consider it as foreshadowing more dangerous self-destructive behavior. We explored how such potentially lethal behaviors were precipitated.

It became clear that the patient acted out his suicidal attempts at times when he felt abandoned by the therapist. Sometimes this occurred in response to his being truly neglected, as in those instances in which the therapist was remiss in making correct therapeutic interventions. At other times, the patient responded to the subjective sense of abandonment which he experienced when the therapist went on vacation or cancelled an hour because of a clinic holiday.

This time we had a seminar session during which there were no patients present. During that hour Dr. R. wanted to talk some more about his work with that suicidal patient and of his distress about how the therapy had gone. He had indeed begun to take the patient's "gestures" more seriously, now viewing the suicidal behavior as potentially deadly rather than just a matter of histrionics.

This had made Dr. R. feel so uneasy that, to make himself more comfortable with the situation, he had instituted two changes in the treatment set-up. I had suggested increasing the frequency from one to two individual sessions a week. Instead, Dr. R. introduced the patient into a therapy group as a substitute for the suggested second hour.

This therapy group is co-led by a female therapist. Dr. R. described her as "an attractive young woman." She had begun co-therapy work as a student and he had encouraged her to stay on after her training period was over *because he liked her.* He made no mention of her functioning competence as a psychotherapist.

Dr. R.'s other attempt to ease his way in working with this suicidal patient was to arrange some ongoing supervision with a more experienced clinic staff psychotherapist. This therapist, Dr. B., had earlier been in therapy with me and had also participated in that same supervisory seminar many months earlier. According to Dr. R., Dr. B. had recommended that he deal with his anxiety about the patient's suicidal behavior by setting up a new contract. The new stipulation in the therapeutic arrangement was to be that if the patient acted out another suicidal "gesture," therapy was to be terminated!

The patient soon complied with the therapist's wish to get rid of him by attempting another suicidal gesture. He called the therapist, told him of the suicide attempt, and had the individual therapy contract terminated as agreed.

But then the patient showed up for his group therapy session. The co-therapist announced that whatever Dr. R.'s contract with the patient, it certainly did not apply to *her* group therapy contract with the patient. As far as *she* was concerned the patient could remain in group.

Things became more and more sticky and unsatisfactory. Soon the patient left therapy completely. Now Dr. R. was concerned that the patient would surely kill himself.

I raised the question with Dr. R. of what I thought would be a more serious problem. What if the patient did *not* commit suicide but came back seeking therapy instead? Dr. R. was more distressed, and flustered by this prospect. He said he probably wouldn't see the patient.

I suggested that he give himself a chance to think it over. If the patient did come back, perhaps they could work it out in a better way. At this point it all seemed terribly complicated. Dr. R. acknowledged feeling overwhelmed.

I suggested that *if* the patient *did* come back, and *if* Dr. R. *was* willing to consider working with him, I would be willing to set up a consultation with all of them. I told Dr. R. that he could come to my office with the patient, and the co-therapist, and the clinic supervisor. We could meet together but *not* to try to solve any of the problems. Rather we might try to simplify the situation so that we *all* wouldn't have to feel so damned overwhelmed.

Dr. R. said he would think about it. A couple of days later he phoned me. The patient had called and he wanted to set up the supervisory conference I had suggested.

After some arranging of schedules, the conference was set for two weeks hence. In the meantime, Dr. R. came in for a regular weekly supervisory seminar session. At the end of that session he took me aside to let me know that there was one more piece of data he wanted to bring to my attention.

But first let me summarize the projected interrelations briefly, as a setting for this new piece of data. Dr. R., who is someone that I trained in seminar, was going to bring his suicidal patient to my office. This patient had once come to the seminar and therefore had seen me in that context. Dr. R. was also going to bring along Dr. B., his clinic supervisor. Dr. B. had also once been a patient of mine and had for a time attended that seminar as well. Dr. R. would also be bringing along his co-therapist.

Up to that point I knew no more about the co-therapist than the information which I gave above in the earlier description. Now Dr. R. let me know that he wanted to caution me in advance that the co-therapist had earlier been a patient of Dr. R.'s supervisor, Dr. B. What's more, Dr. B. had brought the co-therapist into my seminar as a patient during the time he (Dr. B.) was in supervision with me.

This incestuous supervisory conference took place in my office. The cast included myself, the patient, the therapist (Dr. R.), and his supervisor (Dr. B.). The co-therapist was about five minutes late. We began with my asking Dr.R. to see to it that he told everyone the same story as to why he had wished to arrange this conference.

The identified patient quickly focused the meeting on himself by claiming total blame for what ever had gone wrong. He could see that the meeting was necessitated by how much trouble he was causing all of us. I told him that I felt that he grossly overestimated how dangerous he was to other people. I suggested that if he would shut up and listen for a while he might learn just how arrogant and self-important he was being in crediting himself with responsibility for this entire mess.

The rest of us then spent some time sorting out the impossibly sticky emotional tangle of our ostensibly sane therapeutic network. We examined Dr. R.'s anxious avoidance of his own suicidal wishes as well as his wanting the patient to assure him that his therapist's capacity for intimacy was worth accepting. We looked at the faulty contract suggested by the supervisor and its implications about his and my competitiveness. The co-therapist's difficulty in fighting directly with the therapist and the supervisor were acknowledged, as well as her concern that she was not important enough to keep the patient from committing suicide. We each exposed some of our willful ways of denying the helplessness we feel when we make the mistake of trying to get patients to change their ways.

At first the patient seemed confused. Gradually he began to express a curious combination of relief and dismay. It became increasingly apparent to him that many of the problems in the situation were not only outside the realm of his influence, but even totally beyond his awareness. He expressed surprise, and a substantial decrease in his sense of personal responsibility and guilt. But he also let us all know that he was not at all sure that he liked having so little power to make trouble.

The second of my supervisory interventions necessitated planning a suicide. It was decided that the therapist, Dr. M., should bring her suicidal patient to a supervisory session at my office. Clearly this was being arranged because of Dr. M.'s anxiety about her patient, Penny, threatening suicide.

Penny seemed tense when we met but not nearly so unsettled

as Dr. M. Penny was a young woman of about 20 who had somehow survived a catastrophic personal history, but at the cost of being very crazy and unhappy beneath her veneer of pleasing sociability. Because I seemed interested in hearing about it, she talked of her certainty that she would be dead within the next three weeks. She had already scratched the letters 'D' and 'E' into the skin of her left arm. She need only go on to complete the word by carving the letters 'A' and 'D'. Then the word would be 'DEAD' and so would she. She explained that the voices had told here that this is what she must do.

The more agitated her therapist became, the calmer and more determinedly suicidal Penny seemed. The therapist seemed to be trying to get across to Penny that she should not kill herself because she, the therapist, cared about her. I tried interceding a number of times to unhook the therapist from the dangerous role of rescuer. Where I could, I exposed the destructive sense of power that Penny seemed to be getting out of this reciprocity. It was all to no avail.

So instead I shifted into simply asking the therapist to sit it out and rest and watch while Penny and I talked. Her compliance seemed to come more out of weariness than hopefulness. Nonetheless it gave me the space I needed.

I asked Penny about her suicide plans. I told her that I knew that she didn't always do things well. I wouldn't mind giving her a hand in seeing to it that this time if she wanted to kill herself that she did it just right. Penny was a curious combination of enthusiasm and distrust, glad that I seemed to want to help her, and uneasy as to what the hell I was really up to.

She told me that she planned to kill herself by asphysiation in her automobile. When I questioned her it turned out she would do this simply by turning on the motor, closing windows, and trying to go to sleep. She would first drop some acid, pull off the road, and park with the windows closed and the motor running. That way she could die comfortably and expect her body to be discovered soon (so that her family could be sorry for the way they had treated her).

I told her that I thought her plans were a bit sloppy. I asked her first of all whether or not she understood that unless she became asphyxiated quickly she would have intense headaches from the carbon monoxide poisoning while she was dying. She didn't know this and wondered what she could do about it. I urged her to consider using a rubber hose from the exhaust pipe through the window so that she would be sure to die quickly enough to avoid the headaches. She seemed grateful.

Next I took issue with her wish to take acid. I pointed out to her that if she got into some anxiety about her suicide, that having dropped acid she might be in for a really bad trip that would mess up the pleasure of her dying the way she wanted to. Again she was grateful, asked for suggestions. I urged her to try downers such as barbiturates that would assure her a sense of quiet and well-being as she was dying.

The only other issue was where she would park. I expressed concern about her impulsively unconsidered decision to pull of the road somewhere—anywhere. I pointed out that if she parked too close in where she'd be easily discovered, that she might still be alive when they found her. This would result not only in the possibility that her suicide attempt would be foiled, but that she might have to go through the dreadful unpleasantness of having her stomach pumped because she had taken pills.

"Okay," she replied, she would park way out in the woods.

"No, no," I said in some exasperation. "Can't you do anything right?" I played at scolding. I went on with a rather elaborate fantasy as to what would happen if she were parked all the way out in the woods and was not found for weeks. I talked about putrefaction of the body, the possibility of maggots developing inside her and what a fucking mess she would look like when they came upon her.

This made quite an impression on her. She is most interested in how she will appear to people when they find her dead. She was now able to work out a place where she could park that would be neither so close as to foil her attempt nor so far as to make a mess out of it. I congratulated her on her cooperativeness and on her eagerness to learn. I thought that her suicide plan was now much improved. The therapist seemed confounded by all this. She is hip enough to understand what I was doing, but too willfully attached to the patient and too anxious to avoid her own helplessness to be able to go along with me. To her credit, she did not interfere.

When our time was up I told Penny that I had really enjoyed this experience with her. I hoped her suicide worked out just the way she wanted it to. I understood that she was going to kill herself within the next *three* weeks. Together we had developed an efficient plan for carrying that out, one that really had some style. She said that she really liked being with me and I had given her a great deal. I responded by suggesting that should she want to see me again, she certainly could do so. I invited her if she was still around to come back with the therapist in about *four* weeks. Penny hugged me and left.

Despite my apparently playful detachment during the time I spent with Penny planning her suicide, I found myself quite nervous from time to time in the next three weeks. I became aware that reading local news reports in the daily newspapers had become a dimly aware search for a description of Penny's enactment of our improved suicide plan. Fortunately there was no word of my success in helping her to work out a suicide plan that she could be proud of.

A month after our first encounter, Penny's therapist, Dr., M., contacted me to ask if she and Penny could come to see me for another consultation. I agreed and we set a date a few days later.

When they entered my office Penny's expression was a curious admixture of sheepishness and mischeviousness. The problem that she and her therapist were presenting this time was not that of *her* suicide but of her mother's. It seems that since not committing suicide herself, Penny had begun to become flooded with heretofore repressed memories of her early childhood discovery of her mother's bloody remains. Mother had shot herself in the head, leaving her body as a surprise for the family. Penny was plenty upset with this flood of disturbing long-forgotten memories, and so was her therapist. The therapist was very uncertain as to how to help Penny deal with this material, which of course frightened her as well. Sensibly enough, Dr. M. had chosen simply to try to stick with Penny quietly while she exposed the material, hoping at least that her silence would not be intrusive. While not knowing what to do in the face of new material from a patient is a problem often best met with the therapist's silence, in this case it left Penny feeling abandoned by the good mother once more.

For a while I shifted away from this material and into trying to get a clearer sense of my own role in this affair. In part, my uncertainty stemmed from my complex and contradictory responses to Penny. She charms and frightens me at the same time. She is a lovable twenty-year-old battered child, a cluster of fear and pain embedded in a wistfully spooky flowerchild manner.

I asked Penny where I fit into all of this. She answered, "Why, you're my friend of course."

"That's right," I answered. Nonetheless I asked her to tell me more about it.

With some hesitancy she revealed that I was a special sort of friend, a sort of wonder-friend about whom she would write in her *Book of Thoughts*.

I told her that I was very touched that she wanted to include something about me in her writing, and let her know that she had the same sort of place in my life. Seeing that she had been eyeing my tape recorder with some paranoid uneasiness, I told her that though I usually used it to play music when I was alone, this morning I had dictated some notes on it for a piece that I was writing called "Planning a Suicide." I wanted her to know that she was special enough to me to have a place in the books that I write as well. She was as delighted with my valuing her as I had been with her caring about me.

She and I were sitting on facing recliner-chairs at either edge of the large picture window which dominates my office. Dr. M. was sitting on a couch from which she could see both of us while having a clear view of the trees and sky on which my window opens.

Just as Penny and I were having this touching exchange I saw Dr. M.'s eyes widen and her gaze extend out through the picture window. Following her line of vision I turned toward what had been a cloudy, drizzly sky. I saw that now a magnificent rainbow had appeared.

My response was spontaneous. "Look Penny," I cried, "*We made that.*" Penny smiled and turned with pleasure as though she already knew what she would see. "That's right," she said, "That's *our* rainbow."

Penny was alive and we had made a rainbow. There have been times in my life earlier when that would have been more than enough. Now I want all that I can get.

And so I went on. I said to Penny, "Look, maybe you won't be able to tell me what I want to know. That will have to be all right. I want to ask anyway. If you can, please tell me what my part was in your deciding not to kill yourself."

Penny had no trouble answering the question. She alternates unpredictably between being the super-innocent naif on the one hand, and emerging as the powerful high priestess of secret knowledge on the other.. I just happened to catch her in her knowing state.

She said, "What you did for me that was best, was to be just where I was. Whenever I tell anybody about my craziness, or how unhappy I am, or that I want to kill myself, all they do is criticize. They get scared and they try to change my mind. You didn't criticize. If I wanted to kill myself you said you'd help me to do it. The way you talked to me, I didn't have to feel guilty. So I didn't feel like killing myself any more. Besides I wanted to come with Dr. M. to see you some more."

Chapter III
The Good Guys

There is much which seems contradictory in the life and works of playwright Bertolt Brecht. He set out to be a Communist propagandist, but ended up a poet of Humanism. The non-Communist West distrusted his Communism but was enchanted by his poetry. The Communists in contrast "exploited his political convictions while they regarded his artistic aims and achievements with suspicion."[1]

Brecht's own struggle with these paradoxes is revealed clearly in three plays he wrote during the later 1920's. First he did a school opera titled *He Who Says Yes*. In this "propaganda" theater piece he tells of a schoolteacher and some young men from a remote village who set out together across the mountains to bring back medicine to fight an epidemic.

One of the boys who joins the party wants to find a doctor because his own mother is one of those who has been struck down. Along the way the boy himself falls ill. The others must either give up on their mission or abandon the boy in the wilderness. In accordance with their ancient custom, they ask him if he consents to being left behind.

He answers yes. Rather than suffer a slow death, he asks to be killed. The other members of this mission of mercy accept his decision and throw him into an abyss. The individual is sacrificed for the good of the group.

But the members of the Karl Marx Schule felt that there was no need for the boy to be killed. It made the Marxists seem too heartless.

Characteristically, Brecht rewrote the play. The revised version of *He Who Says Yes* was titled *He Who Says No*. This time the expedition is no longer a search for medicine but a journey of exploration. When the boy falls ill, an old custom is invoked which *demands* that he be thrown into the abyss. This time the boy refuses to consent to die. Instead he argues that old customs must be rethought and replaced with new ways.

Recognizing his wisdom, the group turned back, taking him with them.

Now the Communist critics whom Brecht sought to please found fault with his revising doctrine in order to put one individual's welfare before the well-being of the group. Brecht's attempts to resist dogmatism made him seem too willing a revisionist.

Taking up the same theme yet once more Brecht finally produced a more complex resolution in *The Measures Taken*, one of his best works. This time a group of party workers have returned from an illicit agitation mission in China. They report the elimination of one of the members of their group to a chorus which represents the conscience of the Communist Party. So that judgment can be pronounced on the measure taken, the four agitators are to act out the incidents leading to their decision, each in turn taking the part of the young comrade who was killed.

The flaws in the young man's character turn out to be that he was too compassionate to use the Chinese peasants' suffering for the sake of political agitation. Instead of exploiting their hardship, he alleviated it. As a result he had jeopardized the purpose of the mission. He saw the "error" of his ways but could not help himself. Asking to be eliminated, he was shot and his body disposed of to protect the mission.

The chorus ends up acquitting the agitators, approving the measures taken as being in the interests of the Party. The sympathies of the audience, however, are curiously engaged by the flawed humanistic young comrade whose death seems a travesty. Paradoxically then, the third dramatic treatment of the same version of this theme resulted in approval by the Communist Party while encouraging audience recognition of the problems of totalitarianism.

A second paradox in Brecht's work has to do with the unexpected results of his theory of dramatic technique, what he calls the Alienation Effect (*Der Verfremdungsefekt*). He tries to write his plays in ways which create an atmosphere of scientific impartiality. He interrupts the action again and again so that the actors may step out of role to make didactic speeches to the audience. Props and sets are used in such a way as to keep the playgoer always aware that he is in the theater. It is the intent of Brecht's formalist theater techniques to discourage empathy and identification. He believed that only in this way he could hope to get across the political instruction which his plays were meant to convey.

Ironically, just the opposite is accomplished. We easily identify with the very human frailty of his characters. His deliberately didactic stage techniques bring an unintended air of rollicking zaniness which prevents our taking political slogans more seriously than people.

Finally, there is the paradox of Brecht's topsy-turvy morality. He inverts the high life and the low life, switching around the good guys and the bad guys in an effort to reveal how the Establishment exploits the poor and how society's dregs are victimized, forced into their seemingly destructive patterns.

The hero of *The Threepenny Opera* is Mack the Knife, a thief, a pimp, and a murderer, with the habits of a burgher. He is a balding, paunchy businessman who keeps books and strives for an efficient criminal organization. In contrast the villain, Jonathan Peachum, is a pompous moralizing solid citizen. This "legitimate" small businessman is secretly the king of beggars. He rents artifical limbs, boils, and eye patches to heatlhy men whom he turns out as mock cripples. Playing on the charitable impulses (read "the guilt") of the rich who "create misery but cannot bear to see it," his business thrives. Mackie symbolizes the relationship between crime and business. Peachum "highlights the relationship between the self-seeking Capitalist ethic and the self-abnegating morality of Christianity."[2]

I find that when I watch, listen to, or read Brecht's theater pieces, his playful switching around of the good guys and the bad guys simply make clearer to me that *there are no good guys and no bad guys*. There's nobody here but us people.

Psychotherapists tend to think of themselves as good guys, particularly when they minister to the poor, doing long hours of treatment for relatively low wages. And yet, all therapists know that in seeking alleviation for emotional suffering, the poor get the same kind of service they always get. The help they are offered is always insufficient, often inadequate, and ultimately less geared to their needs than to those of "the good guys." As Brecht points out:

> *The right to happiness is fundamental*
> *And yet how great would be the innovation*
> *Should someone claim and get that right—Hooray!*
> *The thought appeals to my imagination!*
> *But this old world of ours ain't built that way.* [3]

For the most part, the therapists who service the poor in public institutions and agencies are young, inexperienced professionals making their beginners' mistakes on patients who can't afford the services of well-trained professionals. Many of the more seasoned therapists (those who are there to supervise the younger therapists) are less talented, more timid, and unimaginative members of the helping professions. Therapists who are both experienced and capable, and yet dedicated enough to stay on within the anti-therapeutic bureaucratic structures are as rare as they are valuable.

One of the many complicated yet commonplace clinic problems is the abandonment of patients. Many agencies are staffed largely by psychiatric residents, psychological interns, and social work trainees, all of whom remain at the agency no more than one or two years. Those staff members who stay on long enough to develop their skills also develop the wish to work on their own. Eventually most of the more talented ones move out of the mental health agency into the private practice of psychotherapy.

The therapist who leaves the clinic either to go on with his training or to go into private practice usually feels guilty and ashamed of deserting his or her patients. In order to ease his pain the therapist my be tempted to give explanations, make excuses, or bribe the patient he is leaving behind with his good intentions and regrets. The usual result is that the patient is then stuck with unexpressed grief and rage. Bad enough that the patient without enough money to get help in a private practice setting must endure the indignities of clinic administration, low grade service, and cavalier dismissal. Hopefully he should not have to like it as well as lump it.

In the case of one private practice bound therapist whom I am supervising, the patients were making their unhappiness known, if only indirectly. Those who had insurance coverage and could, if they wished, afford to continue seeing the therapist in private practice were not at all sure that they wanted to go on with treatment. Those who had neither the money nor the insurance coverage to make such an option possible insisted that they could not do without continuing therapy with this particular therapist. And one young man decided that the therapist was only leaving the clinic because *he* was such an awful patient to have to put up with.

In supervision the therapist and I looked at the problem in a number of the usual ways, discussing the therapist's feelings, the logistics of such separations, and how to handle the reactions of particular patients. I introduced yet another plan. If the therapist agreed, and if she could get the cooperation of the patients,I sugested that we could all of us meet one time for a couple of hours in my office.

The individual patients did not know each other (with a couple of exceptions of people who were also in group therapy together). I did not know the patients (with the exception of two or three who had been in with the therapist for supervision sessions). The therapist had the advantage of knowing all of us. The patients had in common that each was being abandoned by the same therapist. Perhaps as a community of outcasts they could draw strength from one another so that they might feel entitled to the reactions that they were secretly going through about being so badly treated.

The therapist was scared but excited. Because she was trying to learn all that she could from this experience she readily agreed to try it. I went onto tell her that in the past I had suggested such group comings-together to other therapists who were in the position of going from agency service to private practice. Those therapists who had tried this at the agency with another therapist present (not myself) had reported it to be a useful experience.

I went on to point out that I myself had never met with such a group, neither at the time when as a therapist I had left my own agency to go into private practice, nor as a supervisor of other therapists in this process. But I felt confident that since it had worked for those to whom I had recommended it before, it stood a good chance of working for this therapist and her patients, and more important, for me.

Six of the seven patients showed up with the therapist. The session began with a prolonged silence which turned out to be uncomfortable (for me). Unwilling to tolerate my anxiety about this I began by structuring the situation. I told them that we would meet for an hour and a half with an option of going on for another half hour if we all wanted to. I acknowledged that I knew some of the patients from their having been to see me with the therapist in past seminars. They acknowledged that some of them knew each other through having been in group therapy together.

Once they began talking, conversation quickly turned toward the matter of their feelings about the therapist's leaving the clinic. Despite my prior impressions, it now seemed that all but one of them was seriously considering continuing therapy with the therapist on a private basis. Most of them alluded to hurt and angry feelings but little of this was expressed directly.

After a while people began to open up. Partly this was in response to painful echoes of the earlier family experiences of neglect and abandonment which all this recalled. Soon they began to talk not just as "I" but as "we." Mutual support allowed growing appreciation of what the other had been through in earlier life, exchange of intermittent materials, and clearer and more direct expression either of anger or of grief about the therapist's leaving. Where that was not possible, there was at least acknowledgment of more anger and hurt than the person could seem to get out. This constraint was also often explored in terms of the residue of early family experiences.

A brief note on each of the patients present: 1) One young woman had been in a number of times earlier with the therapist. At those times she had been soulfully desperate about a loss and possible abandonment. Now she was openly angry and seemed to feel better about it. The possibility of going on with some other therapist if she couldn't get the money to continue in private treatment was now an acceptable option for her.

2) Another woman who had been through this trouble had gone to her parents to ask for financial aid in going on with private treatment. She said that it had turned out to be worthwhile because she had found out more clearly where she stood, getting both good and bad things clearer with her parents. By the end of the session she was reconsidering whether or not she really wanted to go on with the therapist. It seemed to be a matter of whether or not the bad feelings could be overcome.

3) The next patient was a willfully self-sustaining person who had "always been able to manage," having adjusted to long years of repeated uprootings as an "Army brat." She could admit to some anger but turned the whole situation to advantage. Having to follow the therapist into another town was a step forward in moving to a better place and getting a better job. My initial interaction with her was misguided. I challenged her about the anger that was clearly there but I couldn't figure out why I didn't understand what was going on. It turned out later that she had carried with her a great deal of unexpressed grief left over from moving from one army camp home and school to the next. Some of this she finally got to in the group, once she considered that she had been given permission to cry.

4) The next patient was a woman who forced a division in the group by becoming the scapegoat. She was the one who wasn't going to talk. She was the one who was not going to go on with therapy even though she had the insurance. She was the one who felt powerless because we were all big and strong and she was weak and little. Indirectly, she attacked me at one point because I could afford not to take all this seriously because I had it so easy. I was very directly confrontational with her, calling her on all of this projected power. I moved with her somewhat into the loneliness in her life, the price of her martyrdom. She ended up saying that though this had been an unpleasant mirror held up to her, she though the experience might be worthwhile. In my

opinion she hasn't gotten very far in therapy and is unlikely to do so while bearing her current set of neurotic attitudes which she sees as virtues rather than problems.

5) One young man felt very helpless with his rage trapped inside though he could cry a good deal about being hurt and abandoned. This quickly related to his stories about a father who was a minister and who was cavalier about the patient's and other people's needs in the family. Father always said it was the will of God that the family should move, or change, or do other things which were painful to the patient. He was also raised by a mother who was so good it was hard to get mad at her and the father never supported him in this. He became clearer about his need to express his rage toward the therapist and understood that he would only be free to do so as he liberated himself from the constraints of his suppressed fury toward his parents.

6) This man was in the curious posture of feeling angry at the therapist for leaving but only because he wanted to be able to leave the therapist before she left him. He discussed this paradox with a good deal of insight and was very positively responsive to my straightforward fighting with some of the other patients.

Some of the exchange centered around my encouraging the patients to challenge the therapist as to her motivation for leaving. She was very clear and straightforward about this, talking about her wish to make more money, to be her own boss, and to do things her own way. She did not hide any of this personal self-seeking in rationalizations of external pressure to make career changes. This allowed the group members to express their anger in concert toward her abandonment of them. They questioned the sincerity of her caring about them if she would leave them for money or for self. This allowed us alternately to explore what it means for each of us to be on his own, to deal with the question of whether someone must do just what we want them to do because they love us, and of the need to be able to hold on to what we can get even if we can't have things our own way.

Toward the end of the session many of the patients were reconsidering whether or not they wanted to go on with this therapist now that they were more open about how angry they felt. This occurred even though they could see that some of the feelings of grief and rage belonged to the past. I encouraged them not to make any final choices at the moment but also supported their clarity about the need to make a practical decision in accordance with their own needs.

They wanted to go on for another session or more. I declined, saying that it wouldn't fit my schedule. Actually, in part, I wanted to leave them with all of this feeling to be worked out in individual therapy sessions. For another thing I didn't want to reveal that I just didn't want to go on lest I draw some of the fire directed toward the therapist as she-who-abandons. In the future, if I do this again, I'd like to try to see it through. I'm curious as to how these things will work out in such a group.

I also suggested that if enough of them go on with private therapy with this therapist that they might try to get her to bring them together in a psychotherapy group, an ongoing one. I told them that this had been a very easy group for me, partly because they had a hidden agenda, a hidden sense of community. Also partly because they really put a lot into it and got a lot out of it. I though they would make a good ongoing therapy group even without a bad guy to gun down.

As time went on I knew that the group would opt for extending into the final half hour. Therefore I stopped them short at 10:30, that is after an hour and a half. Without giving them a chance to summarize where they'd been I asked whether or not they wanted to go on. I insisted that the one uncooperative patient make a personal commitment either to go on or to leave. She chose to stay as well.

Then I used the last half hour to have people sum up an exchange about what they had gotten out of this, as well as what they didn't like about it. I explained that partly it was something I wanted for myself because I was curious about what the experience had been like for them. I also told them that they would certainly solidify their gains by making them clear and having an exchange of ideas about them. When all the patients had had their say I asked the therapist what it had meant for her.

She said she felt very good about it, both in terms of how

much help she had gotten in facilitating the patients' expressing their feelings and how much freer she felt about leaving. She felt more entitled to her own feelings, and much liberated from the trap of being special to the patients or having the patients be special to her.

I then added my own summary of what I felt was going on. That was when I got into telling them how easy a group it had been to run and urging them to consider becoming a psychotherapy group. In response to some criticism I also acknowledged that error of the structuring which I had done in the beginning. Some had liked it and some had not. Nonetheless it was an error on my part born of my own need to make things happen, and of my unwillingness to tolerate my own anxiety at the beginning of the hour.

It was not until later individual supervisory sessions that the therapist worked through her doubts about not being a tough enough person to do this sort of thing for a living for the rest of her life. Time and space was needed for her anger toward me. I had locked her into the target position of looking like a bad guy because her underlying role of good guy required that she accept the "victims'" counterattacks without defending herself.

The therapist in the role of the hidden good guy who must let himself appear to be the villain of the piece is a part not often played well. Try casting it. Nobody wants to play the bad guy. Here is a typical example out of my experience as a therapy supervisor.

The situation would have been complicated even in the absence of Dr. J.'s need to play Jesus. As a participating therapist in one of my supervisory seminars that day he chose to bring in a young woman who is his patient. Her name is Marian.

Originally she had come to see Dr. J. along with her husband. They had sought help in resolving their marital conflict. Dr. J. saw them twice a week for a while. After a time it had become clear that Marian needed some additional therapeutic space for herself. It was Dr. J.'s judgment that this should be as group therapy experience with another therapist who was not working with the couple. He referred Marian to Dr. H., an excellent group therapist whose personality and approach are more detached and less mothering than Dr. J.'s, and who (to complicate matters even more) had been Dr. J.'s own therapist when Dr. J. was a patient.

Over the months, Marian and her husband had resolved their marital conflict by separating. Her husband left therapy. Dr. J. began to work with Marian individually while additionally she continued to see Dr. H. in group.

Both experiences were helpful and rewarding to Marian but she began to complain that she was much happier with Dr. J. than with Dr. H. She saw Dr. H. as being competent but felt pained and punished by what she experienced as his withholding.

A few weeks prior to this seminar session, Dr. J. had responded to her need for more help and more intense work with her personal problems by deciding and suggesting that it would be necessary in his work with Marian to increase the frequency of individual therapy to twice a week. Marian very much wanted this but she said that she simply could not afford to spend that much money on therapy now that she was separated and supporting herself.

In working with this therapist/patient couple in the seminar situation, in a short time I was able to identify intuitively the triangulation that Marian experienced with Dr. H. and Dr. J. as related to a comparable struggle with her parents. I shared with her the fantasy that she must have been drawn toward having an affair as part of the problem in the marriage. She confirmed this and painfully acknowledged that she always seemed to be getting involved in triangles. I played down my role in the seminar to avoid inviting her to act out this triangulation with Dr. J. and me as well.

Dr. J. is a fine therapist who is usually very clear about the separation of his own role and the patient's and the necessity for a clear and straightforward contract. In this instance he seemed to be behaving differently. He was on the one hand telling Marian that in his opinion, for the work to go on meaningfully, she would need to come more often. When she declared that this would be a financial hardship, he tended to dismiss her economic problem in favor of suggesting that she was somehow resisting going along with him for other reasons. At the same time, he would not simply say to her, "Look, this is my professional opinion. If you want to continue to work with me you have to come more often. If you cannot, then we'll have to stop." Instead, he was leaving it open for her misinterpretation.

I suggested that he was unwittingly keeping Marian in a bind by giving her the impression that he was *not* saying that it had to be a certain way to work or else they must terminate. She could then seek the treatment she needed through an agency that offered it at a price she could afford.

Instead, he was giving her the impression that they would stay together forever. It was just a matter of negotiating price. She hung in there either trying to be a good enough girl to get what she wanted or to suffer enough so that he would let her have her way out of sympathy. This part of the work was clarified while Marian was still in the seminar room. After a while I suggested that she leave; that the work to be done which required her participation was complete. That was agreeable to all concerned and Marian left.

Dr. J. seemed troubled and puzzled. He had been working in good faith and only now recognized the sticky bind in which he was encouraging the patient to participate. With usual show of integrity he made himself vulnerable to me and to the other therapists participating in the seminar by revealing that he felt that this was an old problem of *his*, reactivated in the situation with Marian. The reason that he was behaving as he had, had to do with his need for her confirmation of his being good and helpful. This is the problem which comes out of some early painful childhood experiences in Dr. J., a residue which arises when comparable anxieties are aroused in him from time to time.

I said: "I believe that you want to be helpful and I respect that. Perhaps you can be most helpful to Marian if you are willing to do it in secret, that is without her having to know that you're being a good guy. I remember when I was last a patient in therapy. It was at a time when I was struggling with a great deal of anguish about my poor health as expressed in part in the pain of anticipating my death separating me from my children. While I was in therapy at that time I would speak often during my sessions of my anguish about my kids. I remember one day talking about some struggles I'd had with the kids and how good I felt about resolving them. The kids were at that time all teenagers and so of course there were many battles.

"I was trying to make clear to the therapist (that is to myself) how good a father I was. I told of arguing with one of the kids, then later recognizing that I could have handled it a different way, going to my son and apologizing, and somehow repairing any damage that had been done to the relationshp. The therapist pointed out that it was my dependency on the kids rather than the kids depending on me about which I was worried.

"Dr. J., that's the way it is with you and Marian. You're talking about how she needs you and inviting her response to that when you're really operating out of your need for her. My therapist was very helpful at the time in pointing out that adolescence is a time for separation and that if I loved my kids one way to show it would be to let them go. Perhaps the best way to do this would be *not* to resolve every argument but instead to let them experience me as being sometimes unreasonable and cantankerous. It's hard to leave a home that feels too good. If I loved my kids I could offer them the possibility that the world outside, difficult as it might be, could be more appealing than trying to be full grown in a home with a father that was sometimes hard to get along with."

Dr. J. was responsive to what I was saying, experiencing my struggle with my kids as something of a mirror for his struggle with Marian. I shifted metaphors at that point. Perhaps it had to do with my remembering that Dr. J. was raised as a practicing Catholic, and knowing that though he had long since bolted the Church, much that I like about him I experience as Catholicism at its best.

"Perhaps the trouble with you, Dr. J., is that you think it's better to be Jesus than to be Judas. Judas was very important. Without Judas there would have been no crucifixion and Jesus could not have been resurrected and the rest of us saved. All that was called for from Judas was that he arrange Christ's salvation of the world by being willing to appear to be the traitor. This was to be finalized by his willingness to hang himself.

"I suppose one could argue that at least God knew what Judas was doing. After all, He'd given the assignment. If that's so, Dr. J., then you can be assured that at least God knows that you're doing the best work you can for Marian, even if you have to do it in a way that Marian herself resents. And if there is no God, if Judas' assignment was no more than his instructing himself, then Judas would simply have to settle for being good for its own sake. It's a tough business. You know what they say: 'If charity were anonymous, God pity the poor!'"

I went on to talk about some of O. Hobart Mowrer's[4] work. He did a lot of group therapy with ministers. Most of them tried hard to make themselves appear good to those around them, while hiding guilty secrets inside themselves. The price for such performances was that they often ended up feeling awful about themselves.

Mowrer, himself a committed Catholic, sought an answer in the history of the Church. He reminded us of the scriptural foundation for the Confessional in Jesus bestowing upon His Apostles the authority to deal with the sins of men: "And I will give unto thee the keys of the kingdom of Heaven: and whatsoever thou shalt bind on earth shall be bound in heaven; and whatsoever thou shalt loose on earth shall be loosed in heaven,"[5] and more specifically, 'Whose soever sins ye remit, they are remitted unto them; *and* whose soever *sins* yet retain, they are retained.[6]

In earliest Christianity, during the first four hundred years after Christ's coming, personal confession was made in public. Sins were often directed against neighbors in these small communities, and so it was before the offended members that men confessed and did penance.

It was not until the fifth century A.D. that the Confessional was sealed, and sin made a private matter between supplicant and confessor. This opened the Christian community to the forms of corruption against which Martin Luther protested. Focus shifted from confession and reconciliation with other men to private penance and absolution. The sale of indulgences even allowed those with money to buy salvation rather than earn it. Perhaps the most deadly consequence of sealing the Confessional was encouraging everyone to play the good guy in public, whatever his secret roles.

Mowrer tells us that *we are our secrets.*[7] It is no wonder to him that so many people live depleted lives characterized by "neurotic" weakness, anxiety, and pessimism. Do a good deed and we must announce it seeking immediate applause. But let any one of us do something petty or mean, and the temptation is to hide it and even deny it if we can. Whatever bad reviews we might have received becomes an accumulation of bad credits.

Mowrer's suggested remedy is that we reverse the strategy first by admitting to the weaknesses, errors, and follies which might make others see us as a bad guy. At the same time that we accept the hisses and boos which divesting ourselves of these sinful secrets might evoke from others, we must begin to try to hide the charities, virtues, and good deeds which make us look like we should be the ones wearing the white hats. He reminds us of the directions given by Jesus:

Take heed that ye do not your alms before men . . .
Do not sound a trumpet before thee, as the hypocrites
do in the synagogues and in the streets, that they
may have glory of men. Verily I say unto you, They
have their reward. But when thou doest alms, let
not they left hand know what they right hand doeth:
that thine alms may be in secret: and thy Father
which seeth in secret himself shall reward thee openly. [8]

Mowrer's contemporary translation of these directions involves his encouraging patients to confess past misdeeds in groups (particularly in the presence of those they have mistreated). In addition, he urges the concealment of present and future "good works." He goes so far as to advise patients to stop paying fees to professional counselors. Instead they are to try admitting mistakes as they go along. The time and money they ·would have invested in therapy can then instead be used for unannounced "good works" for what he terms "charity by stealth."[9]

Dr. J. would have to decide which course to take himself. True, he could not in good conscience continue to see Marian in a treatment arrangement with sessions too infrequent to accomplish what they set out to do. Instead he could of course see her as often as needed without charging her more money. This would require his willingness to participate in such a charitable work, plus the need to work out not only what this would mean to her in the therapy relationship, but equally important, what it would mean to him. Among other considerations, he would have to attend to how this might further embed them both in the already sticky triangulation with Dr. H. (the good-parent/bad-parent issue).

The therapeutic situation seemed already too complicated to promise to be beneficial to Marian if she was in some way pushed to pay more money for therapy than she can afford. She would be creating new problems as a way of trying to solve old ones.

I asked Dr. J.: "Are you ready, then to set up a simple contract making clear to Marian that the only way that you'll continue to work with her is if she increases the frequency to two sessions a week?"

He said, "Sure, I've already let her know that that would be best for her."

I insisted, "No, that's not what I meant. I mean to try and make it easy for her to leave. If she can't go along with that, if she can't afford to come often enough to resolve the complexity of the therapeutic relationship then are you willing to let her go to wherever the hell she might go."

He was taken aback. In all of this Dr. J. somehow had not quite recognized that the most meaningful therapeutic option of his might be to let her go without her recognizing that he was doing this "for her benefit." In other words, he might help her without her knowing he was helping her.

No one wants to play the villain. But sometimes without the villain, the plot does not get developed; the story does not get told.

Chapter IV
And the Bad Guys

More than a thousand years ago, the Chinese poet Li Po wrote:

Hard is the Journey,,
Hard is the Journey,
So many turnings,
And now where am I?[1]

It seems that men have always asked this question. Many have been tempted to accept answers offered by others. It is hard to resist the invitation to certainty, to right purpose, to making sense of it all by joining forces with collective morality, by becoming one of the good guys.

How much heavier the burden of the outlaw, the anarchist, or the libertine! How much more lonely to make your own way, to go on questioning everything, to say "Yes!" to yourself and so risk everyone else saying "No!" to you. If you are willing to forego reason and tradition rather than miss whatever might be in store for you, surely you will be classed as one of the Bad Guys.

Give way to the temptation to eat of the Fruit of the Tree of Knowledge, to know it all, and out you go. Instead we are pressured to restrain ourselves. "Be good! Don't make trouble! Go take a cold shower!" But as a committed Bad Guy, I say unto you: "Learn to give in to temptation." Ask yourself, "What do *I* feel?" "What do *I* want?" And as you begin to be able to hear the stirrings from within, ask not "Why?" but "Why not?" EVERYTHING IS PERMITTED.

If we are willing to become Bad Guys, we can be guided by a contemporary immorality play by Peter Weiss. The conception is out of Brecht's interplay of many alienating levels of dramatic distance between players and audience, aimed at empowering the playwright to instruct the audience politically. But the emotional sensibility is in direct line from Antonin Artaud's Theater of

Cruelty, in which the play becomes "a weapon to be used to whip up man's irrational forces, so that a collective theatrical event could be turned into a personal and living experience."[2]

First produced in English almost ten years ago, Weiss' play has come to be called *Marat/Sade*. I shall refer to it here by that intimately slashed joining of the names of its two main antagonists, but not without first formally announcing its wonderfully long and compulsively accurate original title: *The Persecution and Assassination of Jean-Paul Marat as Performed by the Inmates of the Asylum of Charenton under the Direction of the Marquis de Sade*.[3]

Within the Asylum, the madmen are to put on a play-within-a-play. As part of their therapy, they are to enact a piece written and directed by a fellow-inmate, the infamous Marquis de Sade, and performed for the entertainment of an audience made up of the wealthy and priveleged Director of the Mental Institution, his wife, and his daughter. The subject of the drama is the murder of Marat by Charlotte Corday during the French Revolution.

The play-within-a-play involves events which took place in 1780. *Marat/Sade* is set in 1808. And we see it now, in our own time. The Asylum audience is disturbed that under Sade's direction, the madmen may be commenting on their own times. We in turn cannot watch the production without calling into question the dehumanizing tyranny and terror of *our* present-day world. Brilliantly, the edges of reality are further hazed by the metatheatrical interplay of audience and players making nothing certain and all things possible.

> At the end of the play the asylum goes beserk; all the actors improvise with the utmost violence and for an instant the stage image is naturalistic and compelling. Nothing, we feel, could ever stop this riot; nothing, we conclude, can ever stop the madness of the world. Yet it was at this moment, in the Royal Shakespeare Theatre version, that a stage manageress walked on to the stage, blew a whistle, and the madness immediately ended. In this action, a conundrum was presented. A second ago, the situation had been hopeless; now it is all over, the actors are pulling off their wigs: of course, it's just a play. So we begin to applaud. But unexpectedly the actors applaud us back, ironically. We react to this by a momentary hostility against them as individuals, and stop clapping. [4]

Standing there at the edge of the apron, virtually impinging upon the spectators, smirking sardonically, even viciously, the inmates continue to clap. Some of the audience, sensing the actors' mockery, leave quickly; some sit and wonder about the identity of the sane and the insane, and about the meaning of revolution. Sade looks on, triumphant. [5]

Today we associate the notorious name of the Marquis de Sade with the clinical terms "sadism" and "sadistic," eschewing any personal identification with such perverted psychopathological cruelty. These terms have become degrading descriptions reserved for mad-dog murderers too alien for good people like ourselves to understand. Even when used more lightly to designate disapproval of our more acceptable community members, these terms of disapprobation warn of a nastiness well beyond the limits of anything we ourselves could ever consider. Any of us might be mean or hurtful on occasion, but we certainly are above enjoying inflicting suffering on another human being.

And "in truth," Sade was indeed a scandalized French aristocrat arrested for brutal excesses such as whipping prostitutes in a brothel. Imprisonment led to the restriction of his active debauchery and consequent intense funnelling of expression of his tumultuous desires and extreme attitudes into pornographic/philosophical writings.

Yet Peter Weiss sets Sade against Marat in his play not as pervert vs. political man, but rather as the extreme individualist over against the revolutionary terrorist. Marat is the classic Marxist wanting to set rational order upon an unjust world by means of force, by being brutal *in order to* then be good to his fellow man. Knowing for sure what is right and what is wrong, Marat is a self-styled Good Guy for whom violence is a moral necessity. Had he been born in the United States in our time, he would have made a dandy Vietnam policy advisor.

Sade will not bow to "higher" moral principles and the rightness of ends justifying means. In a debate with Marat, he says:

Before deciding what is wrong and what is right
first we must find out what we are
I
do not know myself
No sooner have I discovered something
than I begin to doubt it
and I have to destroy it again
What we do is just a shadow of what we want to do
and the only truths we can point to
are the ever-ending truths of our own experience . . .[6]

This metatheatrical vision of Sade's led to his failure as a judge. The French Revolutionaries had released him from prison and appointed him to mete out justice with the power of life and death over those he was to judge. Having fully explored orgiastic cruelty and suffering in his own imagination, he was not tempted to make others suffer in the name of some higher morality, nor could he ever impose the death sentence. He who could enjoy personal cruelty as an intoxicating excess of pleasure withdrew in horror from the State's shedding of blood as the impersonal act of murder justified in the name of Society.

What are we to make of this curious paradox of a man? He was a criminal who injured others, a pervert who scandalized the society of his time, and yet a man with strong personal convictions and integrity. He was fully committed to being "throughly irreligious" but only in that "everything that was not human was foreign to him."[7] Ironically, his only blasphemy was against the artificial codes imposed by the impersonal collective morality of society. He wished instead only to follow Nature. Society would be tolerable only if it evolved to the point where it would forego the close-quarter tyranny of convention in favor of the reasonable anarchy of allowing individual freedom unfettered by prejudices which condemn unconventional sexual practices. Then he was a dangerous pervert. Today he would be a spokesman for the New Morality.

With prescient wisdom, almost twenty-five years ago,

Simone de Beauvoir wrote an essay titled "Must We Burn Sade?"[8] In rereading it to research this chapter, I was astounded to see just how much her vision had influenced my thinking since the time I read the piece as a young seeker so very many years ago. I became aware that I was tearfully grateful to her for having given me permission *not* to need my parents' permission to be whatever I chose to be.

Part of what de Beauvoir has to say is that the deliberate self-corruption of the genuine libertine retains a power and a personal authenticity which is lost to the passively conforming good citizen. As he steps beyond good and evil, the libertine is free to release his imagination in the service of bringing personal meaning to his experience. The issue is *not* whether what he does is right or wrong, but only whether it is freely chosen and his own. Sade would not rule out any desire on the basis of it being "unthinkable."

Everyone has thoughts, feelings, and acts of which he does not approve. Those who deny this must also deny the humanness of being part-ape and part-angel. Sade chose cruelty rather than indifference. He would not concern himself with what "everyone says" or what "they" do or don't do. He sought truth in personal experience. He closed no avenues, opened all doors, questioned all of Society's moral certitudes.

He freed himself from the oppression of conventional morality, from the arbitrary necessity of Right and Wrong, from the fullness of excess. He was extreme in everything. Simone de Beauvoir points out that this holds even in his value to the rest of us when she writes:

> *The supreme value of his testimony lies in its*
> *ability to disturb us. It forces us to re-examine*
> *thoroughly the basic problem which haunts our age*
> *in different forms: the true relation between*
> *man and man.* [9]

One of the metatheatrical values of psychotherapy is that at its best, growth-oriented treatment does the same for the patients as Sades's writings do for his readers. At my best as a therapist I make no attempt to set any final goals for a patient. I really don't care what the patient does outside of the treatment relationship. Despite his attempts to invert the contract, our deal is that I run the treatment and he gets to run his life.

But what I do see as my side of our agreement is to help him to be happier, however he might define a happy life for himself. Part of that job is to make him aware of all of his options so that he is free to choose his path, fully responsible for walking the way of his choice. That task involves my expert attempts to introduce him to his Shadow, to those dimensions of being human which he would disown.

> *The shadow is the negative side of the personality,*
> *not necessarily a bad or undesirable side, but*
> *those aspects of the self which do not fit within*
> *the idealized self-image which we each develop to*
> *make living as an imperfect human being more com-*
> *fortable.*[10]

I have no need for him to *live out* his shadow side, only for him to know it all. He needs to be conscious of it—not because it is necessarily valuable, but because it is his. I invite his attention to this awareness not so that he will change his life, but only so that he comes to know he could.

This introduction to the hidden "bad guy" came about recently in therapy with a young woman with whom I have been working for over a year now in what has been essentially a rewarding productive relationship for both of us. It has, however, always been somewhat low keyed in the expression of feelings on her part. Particularly there has been very little direct show of anger by Sally. When she is resentful she is more likely to express some sense of feeling hurt or of being dissatisfied *with herself.*

She has been living with a man for some months. This relationship is one that they both enjoy although it has rather quickly tapered off from that of intense lovers to what she describes as more of a brother-sister relationship. They enjoy each other's company. They share many activities but she admits that often there are feelings of dissatisfaction which she has about the relationship which she does not express directly.

Along with this she is also now complaining that she seems largely to have lost interest in their sexual activities. She sometimes participates more or less "for him," but most often simply declines because she does not feel like having sex. It is a puzzle for her that most of the time when they do have sex, she enjoys it. The problem seemed to be one of unrecognized power-play involved in the initiation of sex between them.

She describes him as being quite aggressive. He almost always approaches her (although when she is disinclined he accepts her excuses). Because he is always soon ready to approach her again she explains to herself that she never has to initiate sex herself by being seductive or sexually demanding in any way.

In a recent meeting with Sally, I made a therapeutic error toward the end of the session. It occurred during the closing minutes of the hour. She began what I thought was to be a brief, final comment on what we had been discussing. Instead it turned out that she had initiated a long and complicated story which was related to what we had been talking about up to that point.

I interrupted, but did not do it cleanly. That is, I should have said simply, "Our time is up." Instead, I interrupted with an explanation saying, "I thought you were simply about to make a comment on what you had been saying. Now I realize that you have begun a story which you won't have time to finish because it's the end of the hour. So rather than let you get started and then have to interrupt you we'll just stop now."

She left the hour without further comment.

Shortly after this Sally began expressing concern about the physical problems she knows I have in retaining my balance. Setting about to "take care of" me, she proposed that she would not require my coming out to the waiting room to get her at the start of each appointment. I usually listen to music between sessions. It's my practice to turn off the sound system just before heading out to the waiting room to get the next patient. What she began to do was to listen for when the music was turned off and to pop out of the waiting room just as I was coming to the door "to save me the trouble" of coming to get her. Ironically, this attempt to protect me from losing my balance usually threw me off balance by startling me as she came out of the waiting room without warning. Recognizing this Sally laughed embarrassedly about it. In the hallway, at first mistakenly seeing all of this as being outside of the therapeutic context, I simply said to her "Do me a favor. Don't do me any favors."

Sally herself is a practicing psychotherapist. In a subsequent hour she expressed some distress about recently feeling abused by how some of her patients had responded to her having set up a no smoking rule in the group she leads. Their response to her *interrupting* their smoking came in the openly angry form of contempt and verbal abuse of the sort that she herself would never express.

I interpreted this account as an unconscious derivative arising out of the adaptive context of the unfinished transaction in which I had ineptly interrupted her. She had responded with no show of feelings, but had soon begun to be "good" to me in a way that I experienced as assaultive. She responded to my interpretation by being able to relate her preoccupation with the way her patients reacted to her interrupting their activities by acknowledging that she herself had developed somewhat resentful feelings in response to the way that I had interrupted her story at the end of the earlier session. She complained mildly that I had done it in a way that seemed to inhibit her feeling permitted to be angry and to show it.

As is my custom, I immediately confessed (that is, I admit to whatever patients accuse me of doing to them and then explore it with them). As we continued to explore the incident, I commented on how inhibited she was *still* being about her annoyance at being dealt with this way. In response she admitted that at some point she'd had a disturbing fantasy. She could not quite claim it as her own, but rather described it as a thought which just kind of came into her head. She said it was something about having thought for a moment of punching me in the head. She felt guilty and greatly upset by having such a thought.

This is very unusual kind of material for this woman, the sort of feeling which does not fit at all well with her usual image of herself. I encouraged her by treating her admission of this fantasy as an act of trust in our relationship in that she felt safe enough to tell me she had been thinking of doing something so terrible to me. Elaborating on this fantasy a bit she said that she knew that her image of my head was of being fragile like a baby's head (because of the intracranial surgery which I have undergone). She pointed out that she had thought of punching me, not in the mouth, but in the head, feeling that my mouth which had interrupted her was strong and hard to fight, while my head weaker and more vulnerable.

She was quite upset at having had such a thought and did what she could to discredit it. With some urgency she disassociated herself from evil insisting that she was just not the sort of person who has such thoughts.

I responded by acknowledging that she certainly did not think of herself nor usually act like that sort of person. And yet I told her that somehow intuitively I felt that there were more sadistic fantasies that went with her elaborations of the associated bad thought. She thought about it quite seriously and replied, "No, I never have sadistic fantasies." And again, "I guess I'm just not that sort of person."

I suggested to her that while that was clearly not how she experienced herself, it might be useful for her if for a moment she could stand it to *pretend* that she *was* the sort of person she was really not. The idea seemed to appeal to her so long as we both understood she was only pretending and that she was *not* acting out the part of who she *really* was.

Once she let herself into that space she confirmed my interpretation by coming up with some fresh childhood memories. She told of the fun she used to have as a little girl cutting up worms and watching how long they would wriggle and squirm before they died. She had allowed herself this sadistic pleasure for just a little while as a little girl. Soon she generalized from the family miscasting directive as to what sort of person she was allowed to be. It required that she feel that there was something wrong with her if she could enjoy herself without feeling bad about how the worms were suffering. Instead her part called for her to feel that it was unkind. How the worms must be suffering! She began feeling so extraordinarily guilty that soon she had to give up even thinking about doing such things. Today it was worms, tomorrow it could be her parents.

I expressed delight that she could remember a time when, like the rest of us, she had enjoyed the power of being gratuitously cruel. Something about this exchange led her back to some thoughts about the relationship with the man with whom she lives. I suggested that there were comparable feelings underlying her troubled sexual relationships. Her first response was the defensive denial which family pressure had earlier required she establish. Her script did not allow sadistic fantasies toward loved ones. She said no, it's not at all true, in fact, she very much regretted *not* having sexual feelings about the man with whom she lived. Indeed she was quite concerned that he would feel bad about her sexual unresponsiveness.

Again I asked her to pretend that she was not the sort of person she really is, but rather that she imagine herself to be the sort of woman who might get sadistic pleasure out of withholding sex from a man. She began to smile mischievously. It took her a while but with some encouragement on my part she could admit that: "If I were *that sort of woman,* I can imagine enjoying seeing a man being very horny, squirming and pleading when he wanted sex and couldn't get it."

Suddenly she knew that she was that sort of woman as well. She could now own the unconscious fantasy she had been having about her "unfortunate" disinterest in sex with her boyfriend.

Sally moved from that material to some more open expression of closeness and affection for me and was much more expressive in what she had to say about the pleasure of those feelings than she had been up to that point. I suggested to her that we were reliving something of what she was going through with her boyfriend and that she had gone through with her parents. That is, the rule of thumb for her life with her boyfriend might be, "If you don't fight, you don't fuck." So long as she insisted on casting herself as the sort of person who was acceptable to her parents, who could not even think of being resentful in a cruel or vindictive manner, then she would have to bury full expression of her affection and closeness along with those denied bad feelings of sadistic anger.

She seemed uneasy and yet encouraged by the recognition of her expression of sadistic fantasies toward me and began to tolerate the conception that she was indeed the sort of person who could have any sort of fantasies no matter how unacceptable to her parents. When she accepted her shadow side then she could also be a more loving, passionate, emotionally expressive human being than she had been since the time she was a very little girl.

To Simone de Beauvoir's question, "Must we burn Sade?" we must answer, "No!" If anything "bad" is unthinkable, then all passions lose their power. But the question has even broader implication. We must free ourselves from letting anyone else define us. Our best protection against the flawed prodution of a half-life, is the development of an imagination in which all things are possible. For this it is necessary to give up the security of a single known reality. Realities are no more than possibilities:

Cause nightmares are somebody's daydreams
Daydreams are somebody's lies
Lies ain't no harder than telling the truth
Truth is the perfect disguise.[11]

A recent experience with a patient named Beth allowed us to explore our mercurial realities once more. She and I were able to instruct each other lovingly as we have before.

That morning Beth was again struggling with life-long uncertainties. She wanted so much to be sure. She wanted to be able to choose once and for all between her parents' way of doing things and her own. As a matter of fact, she did live her own life, doing things in her own way. Despite this autonomy of action, her need for certainty often resulted in intermittent periods of self-torture following each episode of really free self-expression.

That day there was a poignant tone to her longing for an end to the struggle. She said: "I wish I could find out the answer once and for all. If only I could be sure which way was right."

I quickly cautioned her about the danger of her present position. What if the powers of darkness heard her plea? I warned her that it is very important never to speak such wishes aloud, lest they be heard and granted. She laughed nervously. For she has really always known this.

In her characteristically creative way, she had been struggling with this dilemma by turning it into poetry. She brought out a poem which she had written the day before and to which she hoped to get my reaction. This was no shallow seeking of approval, it was a longing far worse than that, a profound reaching out for validation of the nature of her existence. Her poem, in usual confessional style, was a well-told tale of the haunting images of her anguished past. Within the poem there was an hyponotically assuring quality lulling me to be certain that "This is the way it was." The poem near-ended with the refrain again, telling the way it was. But then the final line disturbingly disenchanted my sense of knowing, making me ask myself: "Or was it?" In her own words it was spoken this way:

> Gypsies
> I don't remember enough about the ransoming back
> it was
>> night then, I'm pretty sure, and
> all of the spider webs had been
> knocked out of the corners
> and it was
>> real homey
>> I smelled
>> coffee brewing off in another room
> and men were trading pictures
> smoking tiny cigars
> talking in deep tones
> and opening the blinds to look out at a streetlight
> now and then
> in between playing a Hungarian game of cards
>> and they talked about

> *the necessity for institutions,*
> *especially the family*
>> *and then some money passed around*
>> *and I heard some gypsy talk*
>> *and thought I saw one of the men*
>> *hide a handkerchief in his pocket*
>> *and then they brought me from there to here*
>> *and I think that was probably*
> *the ransoming back, but then*
> *it might have been the original theft.*[1][2]

Once having come upon the final line, I could understand the entire poem in an entirely new way. Beth was of course also struck with this aspect of her own creation, or so she felt.

Still her longing for certainty tore at her wisdom. "I don't know which was the real way! 'ransoming back' or the 'original theft'?"

I told her that her problem was not so much which reality to choose, but that she felt she had to choose either one, once and for all. I assured her that I believed both versions completely. But then I believe that all of the stories that any of us tell are true.

I suggested to her that when it felt safe, she might take some time to reevaluate her experiences as though her life had *really* been just the way the second version implied. Then once deeply into that version of reality, I suggested she should jump switch back into the first version. Hopefully she would learn to shift back and forth with the natural ease one feels in perceiving the changing figure and ground of those optical illusions which are drawn so that first a vase appears and then two faces, and then the vase again, and then two faces, and so on. Such drawings are of course neither simply a picture of a vase, nor only profile sketches of two faces. Intead they constitute *both* realities even though it is not possible to see more than one at a time.

We talked about how her folks are only able to see *their* own realities, to seem to live them without question, and to destructively discredit other people's alternate ways of experiencing. I told her that "That is one of the reasons why I don't like to treat 'straight' people. I always feel in danger of their making me feel that *I* am crazy. Or else I may try to rob them of *their* song instead."

Beth could relate to this. I wanted to make sure that she did not find herself trapped into sharing what she would experience as a freak's eye view of the world. Such a view seems divided between the establishment on the one hand and us free spirits on the other. I pointed out that when I said I did not like to treat straight people, that included straight hippies as well. In order to concretize what I meant by straight hippies, I told Beth a story about an experience a friend of mine had had the other day.

My friend had been in a sandwich shop waiting in line to order one of their very fine submarines. In front of her in line was a very, very old lady. The young man behind the counter handed the old lady her order. It was a small brown paper sack containing a foil-wrapped sandwich, probably her supper to be eaten silently in some lonely room somewhere.

"That will be fifty-four cents, ma'am," he said.

The old lady stood very still for a moment, her hand inside the bag examining the contents to be sure she knew what she had. She did not seem to notice that the counterman was speaking to her. Seconds later, he spoke more loudly, a touch of irritation in his tone: "I said, that will be fifty-four cents, ma'am."

Without seeming to hear, the old lady picked up her sandwich bag from the counter and turned toward the front of the shop. She moved toward the door slowly and with obviously feeble effort.

The counterman couldn't believe it. By now he was shouting: "Hey, you, that's fifty-four cents you owe me." The old lady continued her turtle-trek toward the exit.

The counterman did not give up. He turned toward his assistant, a big guy, young, but very big. The assistant had blonde shoulder-length hair and that look of combined hipness and innocence which is the sort of visual charm which protects such young freaks. The counterman said: "Go after that lady. She didn't pay her fifty-four cents for a sandwich."

The younger man looked reluctant but after a moment obediently pursued the old lady. She was taking forever to get to the door. By now everyone in the store was watching expectantly to see what would happen next. With just a few long strides the hip young man caught up with her. His confidence suddenly seemed to disappear. He hesitated, uncertain whether or not to lay hands on this fragile figure.

Now he spoke loudly, as if she were deaf (or dumb?). "Hey lady, you forgot to pay your fifty-four cents."

When she neither turned, nor even paused, he seemed to decide that she must be completely deaf. And so he stepped forward and around her, putting his face almost into her face and complained once more: "Fifty-four cents, lady. Fifty-four cents."

The old lady kept going. By now she had reached the door, a trembling hand upon the knob. The long-haired young man turned to the rest of the customers in the shop, a look of pleading and total incredulousness on his now weary face. As he spoke there was both wonder and disbelief in his tone. Loudly and painfully, perhaps to the counterman (if not to the god of all hippies) he bemoaned: "Man, *she's* ripping *us* off!!!"

Beth loved my friend's story. It told so well that I assured her that some time in the future I would surely tell it as my story. By then *it will have happened to me*, though in it it I may appear as the counterman, the young hippie, or even as the very, very old lady.

As to the questions, Beth and I had come to the same answers. Are we the good guys or the bad guys? Our answer is "Yes!" Are our realities the true ones or the false ones? Again our answer is "Yes!"

Being bad ain't that bad. Rather than burn Sade, like Molly Bloom my answer will continue to be:

" . . . and yes I said yes I will Yes."[13]

Chapter V
Stepping In and Out of Character

In life, as in theater, the identity of the actor is transformed by the role he plays, whether played by choice or thrust upon him. When we are very young, we are all most vulnerable to those accidents of history that create the parts we are to play. But a man may be grown and still be in a position to lose his identity (or to find it) in a setting so compelling that his usual way of being falls away before some dramatically-evoked situational role. So it is that in times of life-threatening crisis, whether by fire or flood, a life-long coward may become a leader and rescuer, while a chronic warrior may emerge transformed into a helplessly dependent victim.

Situations may even be demonically designed to rob a man of his identity just so he may be redefined into some pre-engineered role. I remember my own sense of being stripped of who I thought I was. Not having yet been instructed by my then unborn sons, I thought that once I had used up all of my legitimate deferments, as a man of honor I had to accept being drafted into the Army. It was nearer to the end of the Korean War than I knew, when I was assigned to a Combat Infantry Basic Training Unit.

The military directors had eight weeks to retrain me from a more-or-less independent, more-or-less law-abiding civilian into an automatically-obedient professional murderer. Their approach to this, involved stripping away all semblance of who I thought I was, and filling the gaps with props, actions, and lines commensurate with the role they had in mind. They replaced my individually-selected clothes with a same-as-everyone-else uniform, cut my hair to an undistinguished length, took away my name, and replaced it with a number. Their overriding slogan was "Your heart may belong to your mother, but your ass belongs to the Army!" I was treated with contempt, kept under pressure, and driven to exhaustion so that I might make the role transformation from "civilian" into "fighting machine."

Another situation in which a person is particularly vulnerable to role transformation is one in which life seems so painfully ambiguous that he will grasp at any context which offers the illusion of identity, certainty, and stability. A classic example of this suggestibility is described by that master hypnotist and uncommon therapist, Dr. Milton Erickson:

> Just before the meeting, the author was informed that he was to demonstrate hypnosis as the introduction to his lecture by employing as a subject a nurse they had selected who knew nothing about hypnosis nor about the author and who could neither speak nor understand English, and they already knew that I could not speak nor understand Spanish. They had explained privately to her that I was a North American doctor who would need her silent assistance and they informed her of our mutual language handicaps and assured her that she would be fully respected by me. Hence, she was totally unaware of what was expected of her.
>
> This unexpected proposal to the author led to rapid thinking about his past partial uses of pantomime by gesture, facial expressions, etc. This led to the conclusion that this unexpected development offered a unique opportunity. A completely pantomime technique would have to be used, and the subject's own state of mental uncertainty and eagerness to comprehend would effect the same sort of readiness to accept any comprehensible communication by pantomime as is effected by clear-cut definite communications in the Confusion Technique.
>
> She was then brought through a side door to confront me. Silently we looked at each other, and then, as I had done many times previously with seminarians in the United States in seeking out what I consider clinically to be "good responsive" subjects before the beginning of a seminar and hence before I was known to them, I walked toward her briskly and smilingly and extended my right hand and she extended hers. Slowly I shook hands with her, staring her fully in the eyes even as she was doing to me and slowly I ceased smiling. As I let loose of her hand, I did so in an uncertain irregular fashion, slowly withdrawing it, now increasing the pressure slightly with my thumb, then with the little finger, then with the middle finger, always in an uncertain irregular, hesitant manner and finally so gently withdrawing my hand that she would have no clear-cut awareness of just when I had released her hand or at what part of her hand I had last touched. At the same time, I slowly changed the focus of my eyes by altering their convergence, thereby giving her a minimal but appreciable cue that I seemed to be looking not at but through her eyes and off into the distance. Slowly the pupils of her eyes dilated, and as they did so, I gently released her hand completely, leaving it in mid-air in a cataleptic position. A slight upward pressure on the heel of her hand raised it slightly. Then catalepgy was demonstrated in the other arm also and she remained staring unblinkingly.

Slowly I closed my eyes and so did she. I immediately opened my eyes and stepped behind her and began explaining what I had done in English, since most of the audience knew English fairly well. She made no startle response and did not even seem to hear me. I gently touched her ankle and then gently lifted her foot leaving her to stand cataleptically on one leg. One of the doctors knew I had a smattering of German and held up his fist, opened it, saying questioningly, "die Augen." Gently I touched her closed lids and gave a slight upward pressure. She slowly opened them and looked at me with her pupils still dilated. I pointed to my feet, then to her upraised cataleptic foot and signalled a downward movement. She frowned in puzzlement apparently at seeing both her hands and her foot uplifted, then smiled at my downward signal toward her foot only and she put her foot down with what appeared to me to be an expression of some embarrassment or bewilderment. The arm catalepsy remained unchanged. [1]

The woman served only briefly as the subject of a benevolent hypnotist. What then of the unfortunate child who lives amidst all of these vulnerabilities, open to being defined by any accidental role-assignment which offers him the illusion of at last knowing who he is? Picture a person who is not only young and helpless, but one who lives through one life-threatening crisis after another. When a person has been demonically manipulated so that any naturally-given sense of self is stripped away, he must tolerate the seemingly unbearable continuing onslaught of the then unanswerable questions: "Who am I?"

The child, Jean Genet, was such a one. At first he had a certain natural innocence, living in the state of grace of infancy. His biographer, Jean-Paul Sartre, tells us he was at first, "a good little boy, a respectful and gentle child, weaker and smaller than his classmates, but more intelligent."[2] But Genet was illegitimate, a child without a known mother or father, unnamed and unnamable. He did not know who he was.

At age seven, The National Foundling Society placed Genet in the care of a peasant family. He was *in* the family, but not *of* it. As a foundling, Genet finds he is given a place to live and food to eat. These things are *given* not because of who he is but because of who the foster parents are. Everything is merely given, and so everything can be taken away. He, the foundling, is obliged. But the foster family, they are not obliged.

Genet's situation is different from that of the natural children.

They are regular members of the family. Their status is permanent. Their roles are a part of the family structure. If a natural child does not behave as expected, he is told that he must improve because "in our family we behave in this way." But Genet's status is temporary and his role so far is expendable. He is told that he must live up to what is demanded. If not, he must leave the family.

Sartre describes how this child of indefinite identity is gratuitously cast into a lifetime role. The accidental historical definiteness of being *seen by adults* while engaged in an age-appropriate innocent act of petty pilfering tells him who is is at last:

> The child was playing in the kitchen. Suddenly he became aware of his solitude and was seized with anxiety, as usual. So he "absented" himself. Once again, he plunged into a kind of ecstasy. There is now no one in the room. An abandoned consciousness is reflecting utensils. A drawer is opening; a little hand moves forward.
> *Caught in the act.* Someone has entered and is watching him. Beneath this gaze the child comes to himself. He who was not yet anyone suddenly becomes Jean Genet. He feel that he is blinding, deafening; he is a beacon, an alarm that keeps ringing. *Who* is Jean Genet? In a moment the whole village will know. . . The child alone is in ignorance. In a state of fear and shame he continues his signal of distress. Suddenly

> . . . a dizzying word
> From the depths of the world abolishes
>   the beautiful order . . .

> A voice declares publicly: "You're a thief." The child is ten years old . . . .It is the moment of awakening. [3]

> He repeats the magic word: "Thief! I'm a thief!"
> He even looks at himself in the mirror, even talks to himself as to someone else: "You're a thief." [4]

At last he has a role. At last he knows who he is.

And what a thief Jean Genet became! Again and again he stole. Again and again he managed to get caught. He became the failed professional criminal he was instructed to be. Imprisoned repeatedly for stealing, for begging, and for smuggling, he expanded his role of bastard-outcast to include that of homosexual-convict. He wrote his first novel while in prison, and much of his later writing was set in this penal world in which he knew so clearly who he was.

Genet was already a succesful playwright and novelist when in 1948, he insisted on stealing and being caught once more. He was given the permanent engagement of being condemned to life imprisonment. To his dismay, his role as an artist was given priority by influential others. A group of France's most eminent writers interceded on behalf of this chronic offender who was both thief and pederast. Only in France would this have resulted in the pardon by the President of the Republic of a prisoner who was neither wealthy nor politically powerful.

Is it any wonder that Genet's writings offer a kaleidoscope of transformed and transforming identities, a "whirlagig of being and appearance, of the imaginary and the real?"[5] As author and playwright, he betrays his own characters, unmasking them and exposing them. He does so before an audience who by watching find themselves unwittingly revealed.

Of all Genet's writings, I find his play *The Balcony*[6] most compellingly illuminating in its ever shifting ambiguities of who's who? and what's what? The play opens in Madame Irma's House of Illusion. (A traditional French name for a brothel.) In part, the opening stage direction reads:

> On the right wall, a mirror, with a carved
> gilt frame, reflects an unmade bed, which, if the
> room were arranged logically, would be in the first
> rows of the orchestra.[7]

And so, the playgoer at once finds that he himself is in a bawdyhouse.

And what a bawdyhouse it is, this brothel called the Grand Balcony. It is a collection of studios complete with whatever costumes, props, and supernumeraries Madame Irma's customers' scenarios require.

In the studio in which the opening scene takes place, we find a magnificently robed "Bishop," in a miter and gilded cope,

Stepping In and Out of Character 139

confessing a half-naked penitent. He speaks in a high-flown theological language before a sacristy adorned with a Spanish crucifix. He is revealed to be no bishop, but a gasman. The penitent turns out to be no more than a whore confessing make-believe sins. The "Bishop" has paid Madame Irma to set the scene in which he can have the satisfaction of indulging himself in his sex and power fantasies. She has paid the whore to act out the elaborate ritual he requires as a prelude to his screwing.

In clerical garb, he commits sacrilege and defiles the church as he rails against the whore-penitent:

> I wish to be bishop in solitude, for the appear-
> ance alone . . . and in order to destroy all function,
> I want to cause a scandal and fell you up, you slut,
> you bitch, you trollop, you tramp . . .[8]

In order for him to be satisfied, however, his sacrilege must remain a fantasy. No matter how authentic the details of Madame Irma's, some element which relveals that this is all nothing but illusion must show through. And so it is that the bishop is frightened that the penitent's sins might *not* be "only make-believe."

THE WOMAN (*suddenly coy*): And what if my sins were
    real?
THE BISHOP (*in a different, less-theatrical tone*): You're
    mad! I hope you really didn't do all of that!
THE WOMAN: Reality frightens you, doesn't it?
THE BISHOP: If your sins were real, they would be
    crimes, and I'd be in a fine mess.[9]

This is but one of such studios in Madame Irma's house of illusions, the Grand Balcony. In each case the customer acts out his fantasy. In each case someone is paid to act out a supporting role with him, to play it according to the dictates of the customer's perverted scenario.

In another studio, a "Judge" metes out punishment to a girl-thief. Another man, hired to play the "Executioner" helps the Judge to cast the thief as the bad half of life, so that he may imagine himself as the good side.

Still another customer plays the "General," feeling himself loved by his gallant lady steed (played by yet another prostitute). The Grand Balcony is a place where dreams come true. For a price, you can be a lice-ridden tramp whipped by a leather-booted pulchritudinous slave-tamer or a leper cured by the Virgin Mary herself. Here everything is bigger than life. Sex, power, honor, and even misery are magnified here.

Meanwhile, outside the brothel a revolution is raging in the streets. The revolutionaries try to keep their victories pure and real. They make a determined effort to live without illusion. But the hope that there can be a Higher Reality is itself an illusion.

Their chaste Puritan ideal, the wish to put an end to role-playing cannot be. The people want to have bravura figures to worship as a way to have clarity about who is who and what is what. The revolutionaries may conquer the palace, the army, the legislature, and the courts. They will never be able to abolish the old whore-houses.

The sacred offices of Bishop, Judge, and General traditionally honored in the community are being overthrown by the revolutionaries. But you must remember that these are the sacred offices which are traditionally desecrated at the brothel. And so at the same time that they are being overthrown in the city they are being preserved in the whorehouse.

In the city, the Bishop, the Judge, the General, even the Queen have been overthrown. But a fight against the revolution is being led by the Chief of Police. It is he who is the real power in the land; and as tradition dictates, in the brothel as well. It is he who dominates people's minds.

The Chief of Police persuades the whore-house customers to don their costumes and to appear before the public, displayed on the Grand Balcony. Madame Irma herself is urged to dress the part of the "Queen," and to join the array.

When the people see this "costumed" reality, they take these imposters to be the actual figures whose roles they have chosen to play. Only in this way can the people reclaim their illusions and be sure of their own familiar roles. The final irony is that once the "Bishop," the "Judge," and the "General" have to exercise their power in the real world, they grow weary. Nostalgically they long long to return to their illusions which were "truer than life."

In her final curtain speech Madame Irma prepares to relinquish her sovereignty in order to return to running the whore-house once more. She bids the audience farewell, saying:

> You must now go home, where everything—you can
> be quite sure—will be falser than here . . .[10]

In *The Balcony*, as in all of Genet's works, every character plays the role of a character who plays a role. In psychotherapy, the therapist attempts to help the patient to get beyond the needless suffering of miscast roles. Ironically, for this to come about, the patient and the therapist must first take on prescribed roles.

The patient comes for help hoping that the therapist is someone who has the knowledge and the power to know what is wrong and to do what is needed to make things right. Despite many therapists' folksy ways . . , including my own "just another struggling human being" approach . . ., we therapists play our parts in ways that imply as much wisdom and competence as we can effect to support the patient's faith that he has come to the right place.

I am an introverted intuitive psychological type.[11] In meeting a new patient, I need only brief exposure to his words, his manner, and his appearance for my head to be flooded with visions of how he was treated as a child, how he acts in many other kinds of situations, and what his fantasy life is like.

I am not always right about these intuitions, but I *am* always certain. My hunches are clear. They come quickly and often I will express them without attempt at documentation, and at times without my understanding how I know what I know.

This works partly because I am incredibly intuitive. My

perceptive powers seem spooky to other people. I love having them. They don't often frighten me any more.

More crucially, my style works because when I'm into myself and winging it that way, I don't really mind being wrong. I'm so often right in such powerful ways that making a few mistakes just *Grateful* adds to the intrigue. In any event, I expect to be foolish more than once a day for the rest of my life and giving-in to this aspect of my human frailty gives me more freedom to take risks. People who try too hard to avoid being wrong are also less often right than I am.

In my therapy seminars I've had fun developing ways of turning my inevitable errors into new leads. Say that a therapist brings in a new patient. I watch how the patient seats himself, how he introduces himself, what he has to say about being there and how he says it. Suddenly I'm absolutely certain that his father must have let him get away with murder when he was a kid. Five minutes into the session I tell him that and maybe add that even now he seems afraid that he can't count on anyone to straighten him out when he behaves destructively.

The patient looks bewildered, thinks it over a minute, and then answers, "No, it wasn't like that at all. In fact my father was very, very strict." Showman that I am, I wing it, ad libbing to him, "Gee, that's strange. I'm usually right about these things, but with you I sure got it wrong. Can you help me out? What about *you* could have given me that sort of impression, when you father was such a strict guy?"

By then the patient will probably be glad to help me out. He was worried that he would be the only one in the seminar who was going to be exposed as a fuck-up. By now he's delighted to be the one who knows, the one who can help *me* to get it together. So then he reveals that his mother always colluded with him as a child to undermine father's authority. Though father *was* strict, mother did let him get away with murder anyway, he reassures me. So now I'm only half-wrong and he and I have a therapeutic alliance.

Add to this my taking the role of director, the one who assigns the roles. I let the patient know that I know that he already knows all he needs to know to be happier, but I also know that he does not yet know that he knows it, but not to worry because I know just how to teach him to know what he already knows enough to be happier.

I also define the setting and scheduling, the limits of the roles. He meets me on my turf, at times I offer. There are only two rules he must follow: (1) he must pay his bills on time, and (2) he must not hurt me physically or break up the joint. The only rule for me is that I am always to do my best to help him to find ways to be happier (but I will do this in my own ways, never to be explicitly defined).

My role is clear to me, but not quite clear to him. His role is clear to me, but an adventure in exploration for him. Whatever he begins by doing is open to our examination as a previously miscast (neurotic) role.

Of course, I have my own private problems in deciding what I am to do and to be in my relationship with any particular patient. Some of my inclinations will not fit my sense of what it is to do the work of psychotherapy. Sometimes I must ask myself, "When is a therapist . . .?" Being in a recent meeting of a supervisory seminar which I run for other struggling therapists helped get all of this clearer for me.

There were no identified patients in the seminar that day, only myself and the young therapists whom I was supervising. Marcia wanted some help about work with a 19-year-old girl, a patient whom she had brought with her to the seminar some months earlier.

The work had been going well and the patient had finally dared to discuss the terrible experience of having been set on fire by her older brother when she was three years old. In the anguished exploration of the meaning of that shattering long ago event, she had revealed that one aspect of its torturous aftermath was that she remained ashamed of her burn-scarred, disfigured breasts.

In trying to help her with this awful remembrance and painful residue, Marcia asked if the family had ever taken her to a plastic surgeon so that her badly scarred body might be restored. It turned out that no one had been willing to help this girl with this terrible problem any more than they had with the other sorts of unhappiness with which she struggled alone.

Supported by her work with Marcia and by Marcia's concerned inquiry, the patient returned for the next session saying that she was going to do something for herself. She had made an appointment for a consultation with a plastic surgeon. Now she wanted to know whether Marcia would come to the doctor's office with her. She asked her young therapist to be with her in this moment of fear, of shame, and of bold new claim for something for herself.

In the seminar Marcia talked of her dilemma. There was a part of her that wanted very much to go with the patient to the doctor's office. But she questioned her motives, the therapeutic value of her actions on them, the possibility that it would be just some acting out of counter-transference, her fear that this was simply an unhelpful residual of her own care-taking social work training.

Marcia sounded as though she had come to the seminar *not* to have someone answer the question for her, nor to decide for her what she should do. What she wanted was to share her own struggle and to learn how others in the group might have struggled with similar problems in their own work with patients. I acknowledged the clear way in which she was claiming responsibility for what she must do and encouraged her to go ahead and seek out the shared experiences which she hoped to get from the rest of us.

Some of the other therapists described situations in which they had or hadn't stepped out of role at the request of a patient, by intervening (or not) in the patients' lives. One choice had been as simple as deciding whether or not to move the therapy of a young adolescent out of the office and onto the playing field or into the corner drug store. Though the experiences of the other therapists was limited, their regard for Marcia and the seriousness of their struggle with the meaning of their own roles as therapists was not. I made as much space as I could for the sort of help they were giving one another before I offered something of myself.

Finally I decided to share some of my own experiences in

situations in which I had felt very uncertain about when I was being a therapist and when I was being Lord-knows what else. I told first of having treated a young Black woman, a late adolescent separated from her family but still living under the pressures of the ghetto. She was what the District of Columbia legally defines as an "emancipated minor," that is, a person too young to take care of herself, on her own, with no one else willing to help.

In group therapy this patient had described the bind in which she found herself. She was working at a subsistence job in a situation in which her boss, an older man, was outrageously sexually aggressive with her. She wanted to quit and get another job but did not have the money to take time off, find another position, and support herself in the interim.

Because of her cultural background (and my own), I felt distressed that she might be tempted to try prostitution as a temporary solution. I asked her if hustling had occurred to her as a way out of her bind and indeed she admitted that the previous day she had phoned a neighborhood pimp but had hung up before he answered the call. I asked her how much money she would need to make it from the terrible position she was in now to a job which she could be safe and self-sufficient. She said that if she had forty or fifty dollars she was sure she could get herself clear but didn't know anyone who was in a position to help her with that.

Impulsively there in group, I lent her the money myself. She was touched, made her way out of the bind in which she had found herself, and eventually paid the money back to me as she promised she would. I told the seminar participants that in retrospect, what I did as a therapist then, now feels just right, but that at the time I was filled with doubts and questions about what the hell I was up to.

I shared another incident with the seminar group in which I had stepped radically out of role. I had been treating a young woman whose father was suffering from a long-term chronic deteriorative neurological disease. My patient was trying to break with her rather destructive family but felt tied into them by her guilt-ridden loyalty to her father. She often felt that her allegiance amounted to no more than a gesture because her father rarely even recognized her when she visited him. And yet how could she abandon this man if her visits added anything to his empty broken life? If only she could be sure that his medical condition put him beyond her visits having value for him, then she could be free. Her unresolvable uncertainty was equivalent to her monumental guilt. I offered to go with her one Saturday morning to visit her father at the hospital. She had great difficulty believing that anyone would do this freely for her.

At the hospital my previous experience as a clinical psychologist who had done a great deal of work with brain-damaged patients stood me in good stead. I was able to confirm her belief that in his condition her father really didn't know whether she visited him or not, and sadly, never would.

It was a difficult trip for each of us in our own way but I am very glad that I went. She'll never forget it and neither will I. I don't know which was more healing for her: my being able to confirm her judgment of her father's condition and so free her from her family, or my simple willingness to do what I could for her. I only know now that what I did was the right thing for me to do with her at that time.

I also went on to tell the seminar group of times when I had refused to visit patients during their own hospitalizations even when the patient had insisted that it was crucial to his or her well-being. I also told of a time when a patient appeared to have fainted at the end of a therapy session and I had refused to help him up off of the office floor. And, too, I shared some memorable moments when as a patient I had been touched by my own therapist's willingness to step out of the orthodox professional role and to offer me some personal extension and help in moments of my own great need. His refusals "to help" at other times seem equally crucial.

I went on to attempt to instruct the seminar group about what I believe is therapeutically called for when you do step out of a role. Should the therapist decide to change a "parameter of a technique[1][2] of psychotherapy, to break one of his own rules, to do something that he ordinarily does not do with a patient, he must observe certain guidelines.

First of all *any rule can be broken* but *no rule should be broken without good reason. The changing of any parameter should be explored with the patient.* The first answer to a patient's request should be a long enough pause for the patient to understand that this matter is something to be explored. The patient can sometimes be helped to see what his request means by inviting him into the fantasy of what it would be like for him if the therapist said "yes," and then again what kind of experience it would be for him if the therapist said "no."

Once having taken the exploration as far as it seems to be able to go at that point the therapist must then decide whether to act on breaking the rule or not. If he chooses to do so, he must give himself fully to the new way of being with the patient, with the freedom that comes of recognizing that *he need only change this parameter this one time.*

After that one time, without having to make excuses, he can go back to the familiar patterns of working with the patient. He will *not* have to continue to break any particular rule nor will he have to submit to further requests of other sorts.

It is also crucial that *some time after the episode* the patient and the therapist spend as much time as they need in exploring what the experience meant to the patient. As for any particular therapist, it is crucial that he take responsibility for making this critical personal and professional decision for himself, on his own.

I do not know what Marcia will choose to do in this instance with this particular patient. It is enough that whatever her decision, it be done thoughtfully, with compassion, and with the courage of being fully responsible for the way in which she chooses to be with the patient. And should she choose to step out of the traditonal therapist's role, to change a basic parameter of the work, she must do so viewing it as an instance the meaning of which needs to be explored with the patient. And as a singular act which need never be repeated.

The roles I do choose for myself and offer to the patient must be understood as free choices. I will not work with a patient who comes to me under duress. Others may choose to work with patients sent by family or courts, kept in treatment by threats of retaliation for cutting loose. I would feel almost as much uncomfortably bound by the role of the one in authority as I do when I have had to submit to it myself.

When we first meet I understand that the patient-to-be is "shopping" for a therapist, and I let him know that I too am shopping. Our preliminary phone contact (if successful) is set up in terms of my invitation: "Come on in and we'll sit down and talk to see if we like each other enough to want to work together."

It is my practice to choose those patients with whom I would work with as much care as I would choose anyone with whom I plan to spend a continuing and significant part of my life. I often see four or five new patients (whom I refer on to other therapists) before finding someone seeking my help whom I like immediately. He has to be someone whom I wish to get to know and to allow to get to know me, someone I believe will become personally important to me.

This practice yields a peculiar cast to my work as a psychotherapist. Because I am satisfied with the patient as he (or she) is at the outset of our coming together, I have no need to see that person change in any particular way. I wish only that we spend time together in which we reveal ourselves one to the other. As part of our contract I agree to bring my expert skills and the best of my work to helping that person discover what it is he wishes to do and in what ways he makes it difficult for himself to do what he wishes. I'll also help him to learn how he might get beyond his self-limitations so that his life could be happier. But what it is he chooses to do and how he chooses to do it is up to him. I am quite prepared to meet him where he stands, follow where he would go, and help him along the way.

Should he not wish to change, that is of no concern to me. I am in charge of the therapy and he in turn is in charge of his life. I set up the parameters of the therapy so that I can do work that seems meaningful to me. There is enough in my life with which I cannot cope without adding a dimension of futility in my work as well. However, what the patient chooses to do with his or her life does not matter to me. *I do not care what he does!*

What he does will not affect *my* life, nor even the evaluation of my own work. I know that in some instances I do excellent work and even so that patient may not get where he wants to go. And other times, though the quality of my work is less than brilliant, even inept, the patient seems to get a great deal out of our time together.

From the outset of our work together I find the patient sufficient. My present posture is probably most effective with a patient who is too hard on himself. It is as though he need only come and spend time with me without particularly trying to get anywhere. There is no work to be done as such. It is as though he has chosen to take a course at school. My accepting him for study already implies that he gets an "A" in the course on the very first day of the term. Beyond that he need only stay on and see what he may enjoy learning. Nothing need be accomplished. No need to strive to make it. He has already made it. From the very beginning he has received the only judgment which is going to be made, my committed confirmation of his acceptability at the outset.

If the patients I choose also choose me, then we go on to work together. At first many of these people express distrust and disbelief. How could they possibly be acceptable as is? They have great difficulty in coming to terms with the idea that they will be accepted because of *who they are now*, rather than because of *what they have done* in the *past* or *what they will do* in the *future*.

If I want to work with someone, I make it clear up front that I already like him. I also make it clear that I do not know exactly why I like him. My feelings are not usually logically or practically grounded enough to explain even if I wanted to do so. At the same time I let him know how sure I am of my feelings and of my belief in the promise of our relationship. This is no pollyannaish dream. It may be stated as flat-footedly as: 'There are ways in which it will probably be very sticky to work with you. You're as stubborn and as arrogant as I am. But I would really like to get to know you better. It feels so good being with you that I believe it will be worthwhile for me."

He's been hurt before. He must have time to try it out. He'd like to be able to trust me. It's only later he will discover that being able to trust is sometimes more frightening than being paranoid. Once he finds out that my caring does not depend on what he does, he begins to experience just how helpless he really is. So long as he holds on to the neurotic illusion that he can make someone love him, he can keep on trying (no matter how unhappy it makes him). He can bribe or intimidate people but he can't control how they will feel about him of their own free will once they get to know him.

Once that's clear, there's no point in trying to be good. He can't get love that way. No point in trying to be bad either for that matter. He certainly can't retaliate against me by fucking up. I wasn't trying to get him to achieve anything to begin with.

Needless to say, there are some patients with whom I never get this far. With some I'm so turned off by my first contacts (even by the telephone inquiry), that I send them away before we have a chance to get into each other. Others fire me during the first interview.

I received a telephone call at the office just this week, from a woman seeking a psychotherapist. She spoke in hushed, dramatic tones. I reacted as though it were a routine seeking of appointment. I had an open hour, so I offered to meet with her.

She insisted that before we make an appointment there was something of utmost importance that she must communicate. She said: "I must be sure that you understand just why *I* have come to *you*. I had been in psychoanalysis for six years and it was going quite well. Then suddenly my analyst became ill and we had to discontinue. We agreed that I should go on with my treatment with someone else. But not just anyone else. In order to find just the right psychotherapist, I wanted to make sure I chose one who was a follower of Martin Buber. And so I contacted Professor F. [a well-known existential writer who would know the followers from the non-followers]. He told me that if I was to be in Washington, you were the one I must see."

I answered: "That's fine. Would you like an appointment?"

She went on even more insistently, the theatrical quality of her delivery rising to the occasion. She insisted: "But it must be very clear first. You see, you must understand that I am an artist of great sensitivity." (With great reverence, she went on to describe her career as an artist.) "And so of course I must have just the right psychoanalyst, one who will appreciate the importance of my artistry, I must have an analyst who is competent, very sensitive and *worthy!*."

I did not say anything.

"Before setting up the appointment," she went on, "I must have your response to what I have said so that I may be sure that you are the one to accompany me on my personal quest."

I answered slowly and clearly: "That's a great deal to try to respond to over the phone. However, I'll try to give you my most immediate reactions to what you've said. First of all I'm sorry to learn that your analyst got sick in the midst of your work with him. That must feel like an awful kick in the head. Next, I want to tell you that I believe that you are wise to be seeking someone who has respect for what you are trying to do that is so important to you.

"But there's more. I want to let you know that you seem to be telling me that you think you are someone who's pretty special. And that you're inviting me to join you so that I may be special too. Every time I accept an invitation like that it turns out to be a drag."

She was furious. "I'm certainly glad that I spoke to you about this before making an appointment with you. You are a hard-hearted man." She hung up on me.

I felt somewhat disturbed, but mainly I felt relieved.

Two days later I received a typed note from her over a piece of calligraphic extravagance, seemingly made out of nothing but capital letters, more of an autograph than a signature. The note read:

Dear Dr. Kopp:
In response to the vindictive and threatened
concepts you expressed this morning I would offer:
Cruelty and helpless laughter will continue to
protect you from those of exceptional personal
authority—as will your choices of people to whom

you feel superior. I doubt your self respect will endanger this safety, unless of course you are confronted personally with ultimate concerns of your own value.

For now, you offer others the opportunity to understand the kinds of psychotherapists who undermine the profession.

What I don't understand is why Professor F. referred such a dud. Perhaps you deserve each other.

For me, the pity of it is, that I would have been happy to have considered taking her on as a patient, if she had responded with any glimmer of perspective. She need only have been able to laugh at herself for a moment, to see us as both capable of being foolish sometimes, to have acknowledged the possibility that we all share some common humanity. Any such show of frailty would have been enough to have invited my interest in making a commitment to work with her.

After all, she and I have similar problems. Clearly, hers is that it's hard for a big star to find just the right director.

Chapter VI
Playing to an Empty House

A man said to the Universe:
"Sir, I exist!"

"However," replied the universe,
"That fact has not created in me
A sense of obligation" [1]

Stephen Crane

Most of us live large portions of our lives as though we were performing on the stage of life. In vain we wait for the applause. Surely there must be an audience out there somewhere! If no one is watching, no one listening, then what would be the point of it all? Living in our own spotlight, we cannot see into the darkness of the empty house. Receiving no response from the empty seats, we assume that we must be a flop. Probably we need to try harder, to improve the show, to wait a bit longer.

Surely *someday* we will be appreciated. If there *were* no audience, no critics to review the performance, then there would be no reason to put on the play. Right? So we just have to go on trying to make it into a hit. We must go on waiting for a response.

Samuel Beckett's characters Didi and Gogo are also waiting, they are *Waiting for Godot*. [2] These two old clownish tramps come from nowhere in particular and seem to have nowhere in particular to go. So they wait, and wait, and wait. The setting of the play is in the simple sameness of the empty world, no more than a country road, a single tree, and always it is evening (a bit late in the day for Godot to be expected to show up). Immersed in the boredom of living in expectation of that which does not come, they find that Nothing happens, no one comes, no one goes. It's awful.

The play begins with Gogo's opening statement of the futility of it all. He says, simply, "Nothing to be done." [3]

Still these characters believe that they have an appointment with Mr. Godot. At the end of the first act, they are told that he cannot make it today, but surely he will come tomorrow. Disappointed once more, they discuss their options:

> Gogo: Well, shall we go? .
> Didi: Yes, let's go.
> *They do not move* [4]

> *Curtain*

Act II involves the same waiting, the same disappointment, the same discussion of leaving, and the same final stage direction, "*They do not move.*"

When Godot's messenger asks what message Didi would like to send, pathetically Didi answers:

> Tell him . . . (*he hesitates*) . . . tell him you
> saw me and that . . . (*he hesitates*) . . . that
> you saw me. [5]

His existence must be witnessed to be worthwhile. Of what use is our act in the absence of an audience?

Because they have defined their existence as a time of waiting (waiting for Godot who will never come), Gogo and Didi do not live their lives for what each moment might provide. Instead they try to find ways to "pass the time," though as Gogo points out: "It would have passed in any case." [6] Nonetheless, nothing matters except the expected arrival of Godot. Life is no more than an intermission. And so they fill the time with word-games, play-acting, arguing, anything to distract themselves from the purposelessness of it all. In the end it all comes to nothing, but because they will not accept that nothing matters, they cannot surrender to the freedom to live as they choose.

> Didi: This is becoming really insignificant.
> Gogo: Not enough.
> *Silence*
> Didi: What about trying them.

Gogo: I've tried everything.
Didi: No, I mean the boots.
Gogo: Would that be a good thing?
Didi: It'd pass the time. (*Gogo hesitates*)
    I assure you, it'd be an occupation.
Gogo: A relaxation.
Didi: A recreation.
Gogo: A relaxation.
Didi: Try.
Gogo: You'll help me?
Didi: I will of course.
Gogo: We don't manage too badly, eh Didi,
    between the two of us?
Didi: Yes yes. Come on, we'll try the left first.
Gogo: We always find something, eh Didi, to give
    us the impression we exist?
Didi: (impatiently). Yes yes, we're magicians.[7]

And so it goes, on and on and on, to pass the time while waiting for Godot. But who or what is Godot? Is he God? Is he Fate? Is he Meaning, First Principle, Higher Purpose? Perhaps Godot is merely a hopeless name for a nameless hope. What if Godot is Nothing? Someone asked Beckett what Godot meant, and surely he should know if anyone could know. Beckett replied: "If I had known, I would have said so in the play."[8]

Yet this question was so insistently debated that soon a "casebook of reviews, reflections and interpretations"[9] of *Waiting for Godot* was published. Sophisticated audiences in Paris, London, and New York had found the meaning and symbolism of this intellectual play completely obscure and incomprehensible.

In only one of the early performances was the meaning of this seemingly bewildering theatrical production immediately grasped by the audience. This performance took place in the North Dining Hall of the Penitentiary at San Quentin![10] The audience consisted of adult male felons, imprisoned convicts for whom that particular play had been chosen largely because there were no women in the cast.

The convicts understood the play. One said: "Godot is society," while another said "He's the outside." A prison teacher who knew the men well pointed out, "They know what is meant by waiting . . . and they knew if Godot finally came, he would only be a disappointment."

I remember my own early years as a therapist on the staff of a prison. Again and again, I asked lifers and other men doing long stretches of flat time: "How the Hell do you manage to get through a sentence of so many years?" The answer was always the same: "How do you pull time on a long stretch? Only one way. One day at a time, Man, one day at a time."

Like Beckett's characters, in a world without ultimate meaning, we are all tempted at times to define our lives in terms of waiting for someone outside of ourselves or something as yet beyond us. For some, this constitutes not merely a temptation of the moment (though perennially repeated) but an essential motif and lifestyle. This waiting is not a bad working definition of neurotic character style.

I have treated many patients whose central longing seems to be for someone who "really" cares. Such people do not focus clearly on whether or not how they live is good for them and makes them happy. They pay less attention to how other people *actually* treat them, than to pursuing that phantom audience, that someone who will *really* love them.

The other day this surfaced very clearly in a woman with whom I have been working for quite a while. She hides her anger often, acts against her own best self-interests, and suffers greatly in this lifelong search for the unobtainable. Yet just this melodrama is her reality.

A clear example came up in her intense pain at the thought that a man *whom she was no longer seeing* might not *really* care about her. She did not want him to care primarily in terms of hoping that he would return to her and make her happy. It would be enough if in their separation, he simply went on caring. This was not the first time that such a tragic love affair had been described by her. It was just the first time that it was so clear, even to her.

I asked her to consider what sort of a world it might be for her if there was no way in which she could ever know if someone *really* cared. Even when she thought someone really cared, then she questioned whether or not they *really*, really cared. She seemed puzzled but interested. I suggested that she seemed less concerned with how she was treated than with being able to maintain the fantasy that it mattered to someone else.

She seemed disturbed by my comments, wondering if I was making fun of her. I assured her that I was not, rather that I was simply trying to understand her experience, it being so different from how I had come to experience life in recent years. She wanted to know just what I meant by that. I went on to tell her that now personally I would rather be treated well by someone who might *not* really care, who might be just manipulating me, than to be treated badly by someone who assured me that he *really* cared. I had had enough of the latter scripting as a child. I made clear to her that I felt that I could never know for sure whether anyone *really* loved me, but that I sure as hell knew when I was being treated well or badly.

Her anxiety led her back to examining *our* relationship. She panicked at the notion that perhaps all this time I had not *really* cared about her but had been just manipulating her. Variations on this theme have come up again and again as she has wondered if how I am treating her in our sessions is an expression of real concern or just some technical manipulation, some theatrical trick of therapy.

I make less and less distinction between the two in my own mind. I asked her then if she would object seriously to my having manipulated her by making her feel loved in order to trick her into being happy. I pointed out that I had no way of knowing whether or not I *really* loved anyone or if anyone *really* loved me. I do know that there are some people whom I enjoy treating very well and that there are other people who seem to enjoy treating me very well. These are the relationships which she might characterize as being *really* loving. All *I* know is that they feel good.

She said that this whole idea "boggled" her mind. As far back as she could remember all her life she had lived to be *really* loved.

"The idea of *really* loving and *really* being loved, that's my treasure. It's my jewel," she said.

My immediate response to her was, "This jewel, can you eat it?" I went on to reveal my fantasy about her being downed in the jungle in a plane crash with a number of other people. She was carrying a sack of jewels. I wondered how long it would take her to trade them for a tuna fish sandwich.

She backed off as if in response to blasphemy. I asked, "Do you think I'm being too sentimental?" She broke up. The laughter went on and on.

It may well be that "Psychoanalysis is the disease for which it pretends to be the cure."[11] In the same way we can be misled by Aristotle's touting of the cathartic value of experiencing the tragic suffering of serious-minded supervirtuous heroes. Identifying with these better-than-ordinary tragic figures provides less relief for us ordinary folk than the common humanity we find with pathetic comic characters like ourselves stuck in a world that makes no sense. Comedy, not tragedy, is the crucial emotional release, the metatheater of freedom.

The origins of such neurotic seeking of someone who *really* loves them come about in people who in the first few years of life have had a brief experience of continuous good mothering (from either parent). At some point the mothering-parent loses interest, turns to another child, or simply rejects the loved child. For the child there seems to be no reason for this abandonment.

The arbitrariness of the loss is too painful a conception for a helplessly dependent child to bear. Rather than accept that this is a parent who has given her up for no good reason, the child begins to feel that there is something wrong with her. She may spend a lifetime blaming herself, trying to find out what is wrong with her, trying to be the sort of person who will be *really* loved once more.

The experience of passing through a great deal of grieving and pain is necessary before such a person can accept that there is no way of knowing for sure whether she was ever *really* loved. Enough that she got some good treatment for a while. The betrayal experienced in the mothering-parent's loss of interest in her must be faced.

The initial loving had been accepted in all innocence as a state of grace. Suddenly she had to live in a world in which the experience of being *really* loved was lost. In the face of the questions, "Was I really loved? Was I fooled? Did I fool myself?" there follows a life of searching for the experience of being really loved again, the search for someone who really cares.

The fear of betrayal born of the first abandonment, bolstered by the feeling that the patient was herself to blame, leads to perennial distrust of whatever is given. The final irony is that at least momentarily such a patient is more likely to feel *really* loved by someone who is erratic in how he treats her. Being treated very well in a continuing way is something that the patient finds hard to bear without the bitter-sweet experience of the grief of love once had and now lost.

Being treated well means that rejection may constitute the next scene. Can this truly be love? Being treated sometimes well and sometimes badly can be linked to the person's feeling that she must have done something wrong. Perhaps this person who often treats her badly is the one who really loves her. My patient's emphasis on whether someone who has left her really cares is a fantasy restoration of the early felt genuineness of the love of the deserting parent.

The therapist is not Godot. Therapy will not provide salvation, will not offer that stroke of grace of once more finding someone who *really* loves her. The position of the therapist is well stated in another of Beckett's plays, in which one of the characters tells:

> . . . the story (of a new mind doctor and) of a little girl, very unhappy in her ways, and how he treated her unsuccessfully over a period of years and was finally obliged to give up the case. He could find nothing wrong with her, he said. The only thing wrong with her as far as he could see was that she was dying. And she did in fact die, shortly after he washed his hands of her.[12]

What my patient finally came to was that in the absence of someone *really* loving her, nothing would matter. I told of a friend who was a devout Catholic, a woman who had not missed a Mass in twenty years. Once I asked my friend what it would mean to her if there was some way that she could discover that indeed there was no God. Without hesitation she said that "Nothing in the world would mean anything then. I would probably kill myself."

My patient too feared the absence of meaning in her life. She was surprised to find that what she feared most was freedom. As she put it, "If I discovered that nothing really mattered, then I would have to do whatever I wanted to do." We agreed that she already did know this but at the moment it was just too frightening to tolerate.

Despite the anguish of the futile seeking of certainty that someone *really* loves her, this tragic role has been familiar misery for the patient. It hurts a great deal but she feels very special and important as she suffers through it. The experience is familiar. She's had it almost all of her life. At least she knows how to handle it. Should she give up waiting for Godot, she would find herself beyond the comfortably painful limits within which she lives. Nothing would be certain. All would be possible. Nothing would matter and so she would have to bring meaning to her own life. She could become the one who really cared about what happened to her. She might as well. No one else cares as much about her as they do about themselves. As my wife, Marjorie, says so clearly, "I guess one of the things being an adult means is that you're the only one who can judge how you're doing. No one else's judgment really counts for much."

When you find out that everything is useless, you can stop struggling against the tide, stop trying so damn hard, and enjoy yourself. The patient already knows all of this and wishes she did not. There is no Godot. The hope of salvation through the workings of grace is an empty dream. But as with the two thieves at the crucifixion of our Lord, salvation is a 50-50 chance. As Didi points out, "It's a reasonable percentage."[13]

Some aspects of my own tragic seeking of an appreciative audience are not entirely unlike those of my patient. The main difference is that my early state of grace was not a feeling of being *really* loved so much as an experience of being *really* admired.

Clearly I was too bad ever to be loveable, but I was so smart my father could not seem to help but admire me.

Still another piece of this struggle was worked-through a few years ago with the creative restaging help of a man running a Gestalt weekend workshop for which I had signed up. That man is Erv Polster, an old friend, a talented therapist, and a lovely human being.

Ostensibly I went there so that an experience with Erv could instruct me. Facing my anxiety of re-entering a new group situation, unwittingly I fell back upon old defensive ploys. Soon I found myself assisting Erv in running the group rather than simply being a participant member (the role in which I had paid to be cast.)

Erv became aware of what I was up to and helped me to get in touch with what it was all about for myself. In our dialogue it became clear, that though I knew better, I was still seeking some confirming recognition. Erv said that (if I would trust him for a few minutes) he would help me (if I wished) to get into more immediate contact with what was going on inside me. I immediately agreed, partly because I trust Erv and partly in a further need to show off to the audience that I could do anything.

Erv said that all that I would need to do would be to sit quietly for five minutes and pay attention while the whole group applauded me. I said, "Sure, fine" (after all, I ought to be able to do anything for just five minutes). It all sounded innocuous enough. The group was curious. Having found Erv's suggestions imaginative and helpful up till then, they agreed to participate by playing the part of the applauding audience.

All eyes turned toward me. The sound of both hands clapping generated by each of the other people in the room began to merge and swell, to come rolling in over me like waves of approval. The sound fit well with everyone's leaning forward, smiling appreciatively, and moving as though enjoying giving a gift.

At first I simply felt amused. The more absurd it all seemed, the harder I laughed. Then came a sense of the soft pleasure of feeling appreciated. I knew that Erv's appreciation of me was personal and genuine.

But embarrassingly I also found that even the mock applause of the group was somehow satisfying. I grew uncomfortable at seeing that my inner longings for admiration could be appeased by such an obviously contrived piece of business.

What came next was far, far worse. My belly felt uncomfortably hot and full. As the sensation rose up into my chest it became at the same time more diffuse and more distressing. All at once the aching in my chest had a voice. It spoke to me of how long I had gone without feeling that anything I did was enough to make me feel that I meant anything at all to myself or to anyone else.

I had the flash of an image of my father taking me to the Museum of Natural History when I was a very, very little boy. He warmed me with a smile of pleasure and pride in how hungrily bright a child I was. Crazily, I felt that no one had ever again smiled at me like that *till now.*

I cried out in anguish over paradise lost. There was no suppressing the pain now. The applause continued as I sobbed and sobbed and sobbed. A trusted friend sat beside me in the group, she too still applauding. Wisely I pleaded with her to please stop clapping and to hold me instead. She did. I went on crying, I don't have any idea for how long. It was only later on that I became clearer about how much more important it is for me to give up (as best I can) what's left of the ways in which I show off and impress so that someone else will *really* admire me. I must remember to remember to pay attention to how I want to be treated, to ask for it more directly, and to judge what I get in terms of how it *feels to me* rather than by what I imagine it *means to them.*

I must define myself. To ask others to define me, no matter how kind and trustworthy they may be, is to do myself in. It seems likely to me that anyone who would join me in this act seeks only that my reciprocity define him as well. I ask that he be my audience. He agrees only to have negotiated a co-starring role, or worse yet, to unwittingly define me as *his* audience in turn.

Didi and Gogo are each in some ways only half-men. If Godot really exists, he is likely to define himself in terms of their waiting as they define themselves in terms of his coming.

There are ways in which these two characters may be seen as living the polar half-lives of dreamer and realist, poet and pragmatist, even as caricatures of mind and body. Between them, they might make a single hero.

There are as well in Beckett's play a pair of secondary characters, who live out a more clearly interdependent love-hate relationship. Without ever really being satisfied with the arrangement, Pozzo and Luck define themselves as slave and master. Each has found his Godot. In any of these characters we may find ourselves. The search for certainty, for being something to someone else, limits our chances to become who we are to ourselves. I consider myself fortunate to have continuing help in this matter from the patients I treat and from witnessing my young son's struggles to resist yielding to the temptation to let others define who they are. A recent epiphany emerged through the irreverent instruction of my youngest son.

It was several weeks past my son Nick's sixteenth birthday. He had taken his driving test several times without managing to pass. There was no part of it which he was unable to master. He just wasn't seeming to get all the parts right at any one time.

He was obviously upset and frustrated by these experiences, but typically seemed to feel that there was no point in talking about it very much. Now he had finally passed the test and he had lots and lots to say. He was very excited, very pleased, but had also gotten around to spewing forth the heretofore unexpressed bad feelings as well.

Each time he seemed to come to a point where he felt he had said about as much as anyone might be ready to listen to, I encouraged him to go on with my own random comments, such as "Gee, it sure must feel good to finally pass!" or "Well, you won't have to go through that one again!" He was looking forward to all the final freedom that driving would bring to him, while at the same time revealing how hard it had been for him up to now.

He had been tense, worried that he might never pass, and sleepless the night preceding each examination. All of this anticipatory uneasiness made it even harder for him to pass each subsequent test. But this time he had passed! He explained his success to himself in terms of having psyched himself up before taking today's test. He explained that it was the sort of thing that he did when he played football in order to take on offensive linemen who might be bigger or stronger than he considered himself to be.

Although usually not at all given to psychologising or to theoretical discussion, that triumphant day Nick seemed very much interested in talking to me about my understanding as a psychologist of the problems of mind over matter.

We talked about whether or not "insane people" were stronger than "normal people," how hypnosis really worked, and the relationship between Oriental religious attitudes and the Kung Fu martial arts.

In an effort to communicate some of this material on a personal level, I described to him some help I had gotten with the chronic headaches I must endure. I told him of how a Gestalt therapist named Joen Fagan, at an American Academy of Psychotherapists workshop had taught me to induce controlled hallucination in a way which allowed me to move the site of a focal headache within my head in an effort to control and free myself of the pain.

I also told him of the work she had done with a young woman who had a severe case of poison ivy. Joen had taught her to hallucinate moving the poison ivy itch to another place on her body. In this way she could scratch the itch in places in which she had no poison ivy and so relieve herself of discomfort without spreading the irritation.

Nick was fascinated. The effectiveness of psyching himself up in the sports arena was the soundest reality support he could be given for almost anything. But he complained that mind over matter didn't always seem to work. Recently, the afternoon before he was to take a driving test the next morning, he discovered that he had a severe headache (apparently from the anticipatory tension). Instead of taking a couple of aspirin and resting, he went off to basketball practice, trying to psych himself out of the headache. It didn't get any better. He of course persisted in playing ball and came home feeling awful.

I pointed out that one of the ways in which I had dealt with my own headaches was to give in to them. I have found that most often I simply could not *overcome* the pain. What's more, fighting against it seemed to increase the pain. It was like working against myself.

Finally, in a playful way I pontificated to him, saying: "Look Nick, there are some things you just have to learn to get used to. There are two things in life that you can't psych yourself out to overcome, two things in life to which you just have to surrender. One is a headache and the other is my authority over you as a father."

Nick turned to me with his super-lovable grin. Without a moment's hesitation, he replied: "Well, dad, one out of two ain't bad."

Our two older sons went on to complete my latest lesson in the need for each of us to maintain the integrity of his own individual reality. Each member of our family seems to have something of his or her own going for him (or her). But of course each one's crown is also his cross. We each appreciate the other's outstanding talents, and of course we each resent them.

David, age 18, is clearly far and away the brightest member of the family. He knew this long before any of the rest of us were ready to acknowledge it. He's long been bored in school, but always interesting to talk to. He has served as the family's encyclopedia but irritatingly he can also be experienced as talking down to any one of us at any given time.

When he was sixteen (and I was forty-three) we were having one of our struggles. He interrupted to straighten me out. "Dad," he explained, "the reason we're having so much trouble in settling this disagreement is that I'm much brighter than you are. Of course as my father it's hard for you to accept that. You're certainly very bright in your own right," he went on, "bright enough to do most things that you want to do. But your denial of my being brighter than you are, plus your overestimation of the importance of experience, makes it hard for you to credit some of my premises as being more developed and relevant than your own."

Like all other family struggles, this goes on with variations for as long as the family continues to be together. Recently, both Jon and David have moved out of the house to continue their educations at colleges in other cities. When they come home to visit there is much in the way of evaluative restructuring as both they and we struggle to explore the changes in our relationships with each other.

During a recent home visit, when we were all seated around the dining room table after supper one night, David had once more taken on the whole family. But this time much of the conflict was explicitly between Jon and David. David complained loudly, saying "Look, Jon, I know that as my older brother it would be very hard for you to acknowledge that I am brighter than you are. My being brighter doesn't mean that I'm necessary right in this particular instance, but I really get tired of being put down on the basis of being younger without being respected for being.

Jon seemed to stop to think it over. Finally he turned to David and said: "This is hard for me to say, David, because you *are* my younger brother. What's more you've almost always been bigger than I am physically. I may be making myself vulnerable in a way that I will later regret but I feel that I should say to you that I do recognize that you are much brighter than I am."

David looked stunned, but very pleased. He smiled and savored Jon's response. But this new state of affairs was only to last but briefly.

Jon went on: "You're much more intelligent than I am all right, David," said Jon. "But I guess being very intelligent is not *that* important to me. If I had to pick between being super-smart, and being sensitive to where I am in my relationships with other people, I'd certainly pick the psychological sensitivity rather than the developed intellect."

David recovered in moments. "I guess that's just the way it is," he responded. "We each value most whatever we do best." Again I had been instructed in what we each must learn. David was telling us that we must each come to know that "I am the best possible version of me there is—if only I will acknowledge it, love it, and nourish it."

Again David had demonstrated that we each must witness for ourselves. Other people may matter to us in their own way, but no one else can define the meaning of our lives for us. The subject of Beckett's play is not Godot, but waiting. We must live our lives in the freedom of the absence of outside judgment.

Godot and the assurance that someone else will *really* love us, *really* appreciate us, is never more real than a broken promise. Every such hope is a lie. Sometimes, like Didi, my patients complain, "This is becoming really insignificant." Then as the therapist, like Gogo, I must answer, "Not enough." In that empty space lies our only hope.

The most important struggle takes place within ourselves. Again and again we each must choose between being and pretending, between gesture and futility, between a staged performance and an improvised life. When it works, therapy allows the patient to give up pretending, to forsake his audience, so that he may go on with the business of living a life that can never mean as much to anyone else as it means to him. It is tempting to sacrifice spontaneity and stick to the script. Yet we must give up asking others, "When will Godot arrive?" Instead we must ask ourselves, "What the hell are we doing here waiting?"

Part III
Tragedy and Beyond

Chapter I
The Tragic Hero

Some common experiences seem a fundamental part of every human being's sense of life, but tragedy is *not* one of them. Compare the concept of the *tragic* with the idea of the *holy*.[1] Almost every language has a word for the experiences of "the holy." All over the world we find this concept, not as a designation spread from a common linguistic source by cultural diffusion, but rather as a term arising out of the need of every group of people to describe a universal human experience.

This is not the case with the term, "tragic." Tragedy is no more than an early Western form of literature which fits well our particular now-failing cultural legacy, but remains no more than a literary conceit nonetheless. The term did *not* arise out of humanity's cradle to describe some basic common human phenomenon. It does *not* appear everywhere. It is *not* the way of Everyman.

Tragedy was originally a sixth century B.C. Greek word, coined in Athens some 2500 years ago to describe a particular kind of play then in vogue upon the stage in that ancient city-state. No other language has a word for "tragic," except insofar as it has been taken over and adapted from the original Greek theater term. Tragedy, like nationalism, is a costly and burdensome evaluative elaboration, a cultural device and a historical extravagance rather than a biological necessity. It is an inessential and limiting category of interpretation whose time has passed.[2]

The phenomenon of *theater* itself does appear everywhere, even in the rites of the earliest primitive communities. Shamans and worshippers, dressed in animal skins, chant and dance, as they perform ritual portrayals of the birth and death and resurrection of gods and spirits. True enough, the modern conception of theater in the history of Western Civilization begins in the first great theatrical age of sixth century B.C. Athens.[3] It is there that the three elements of what we have come to call theater first emerged: actors who sing or speak independent of the original unison chorus; dialogue which conveys an element of conflict; and an audience whose participation in the action is limited to its emotional involvement.

It was in this age of the glory that was Greece that actors first performed in place of priests, in hallowed places set aside for those performances, yet in places which were not temples. It was there that the classic tragedies of bold Aeschylus, skilled Sophocles, and subtle Euripides were conceived, written, and performed.

These roots of modern theater developed gradually in classical Athens, beginning as the unison singing of hymns around the altar of Dionysus, the mad wine-god of frenzy and abandon. It was Thespis who first detached himself from the chorus to play out the part of the god whose deeds were being celebrated. So it is that even today, actors are called thespians.

Aeschylus added a second character, introduced dialogue and thus reduced the importance of the chorus. Sophocles went on to add yet a third character, increased the dialogue still further, and transformed each play of the customary triology into an organic unit. Euripides made the characters and plots more complex, introducing social, political, and philosophical issues, as well as beginning the shift from characters who were mere pawns of Fate or divine power, to those human beings in conflict in more psychological dramas.

These three playwrights (whose surviving works make up the bulk of our treasured residue of that first great age of theater) were contestants in a dramatic competition. Their official title was *tragoidoi*, a term which refers to a goat song. The derivation of this term has been variously attributed to the fact that the original prize at these sacred festival drama contests was a goat to be won by the author of the best play (song); that the original chorus consisted of satyrs who wore the skins of goats (the sacred animals of Dionysius); or that the word comes from the Dionysian attendants whose half-goat/half-man antics enlivened the interspersed Satyr plays which offered comic relief between the tragic triologies.

Still, it is true that the original tragic plays are thematically related to our later use of the term in that it is the good who fall from grace. Tragedy is a form of literature concerned with "noble suffering," a dramatic convention which "aims at representing men . . . as better than in actual life,"[4] as better than ordinary men. Tragedy "is a paradoxical combination of a fearful sense of rightness (the hero must fall) and a pitying sense of wrongness (it is too bad that he falls)."[5]

The dreadful necessity of the distressing consequences of the actions of tragic heroes are often known to them in advance. Often Fate (*deus ex machina*) seemingly serves to administer the eventual punishment, but it is the action of the hero himself which actually leads to his being thrown by his own weight, while "the gods are, in effect, the natural or inevitable course of things."[6]

So it is that Fate draws the hero (or heroine) toward his (or her) awful end by means of some "tragic flaw" of character. The fatal weakness is most often an excess of some virtue, such as pride or determination. The tragic hero "always gets what he wants—and always pays the full price."[7] He appears to disturb some natural balance which always rights itself by the final scene. Thus tragedy tells a bit more than the truth in its exaggerated emphasis on nobility, duty, virtue, the fall of the mighty from grace, and the inevitable restoration of natural order.

Like the contemporary neurotic men and women who seek my help in psychotherapy, the heroes and heroines of classical Greek tragedy see themselves as especially selected victims of cruel fate, made to suffer by ineluctable necessity. It is, they feel, because they are somehow too good, too committed to some inexorable higher value. They lack, not self-consciousness, but perspective and humor, as they take themselves and their situations too seriously, and the absurdity of life not seriously enough. And so they cannot but participate in their own unhappy dramatizations, but they feel that they do so somehow through no real fault of their own.

For me Freud's most convincing counsel concerning what a psychotherapist could do for a patient is:

No doubt fate would find it easier than I to relieve you of your illness, but you will be able to convince yourself that much will be gained if we succeed in transforming your hysterical misery into common unhappiness.[8]

Freud's point is, in part, that life by its very nature involves some frustration, pain and disappointment. But it is not the nature of life but of neurosis that elevates such universal, everyday bits of unhappiness to the tragic extreme of "hysterical misery." The stubborn, self-willed, insistence of the neurotic is not a tragic flaw of character, but a way of behaving, a soluble problem brought about by his having been too early and too often faced with more pressure and less caring than he could endure. As a psychotherapy patient, he has the opportunity to spend time in a safer, non-blaming, and yet more confronting relationship. Here he gets a second chance, in the form of an opportunity to correct earlier miscasting and to revise bad scripts. He may now learn to alternate flexibly between acting and directing, between rehearsed performances and spontaneous ad libbing, as he increases his ability to improvise and enlarges the repertoire of his life.

Like the "tragedy" of neurotic life style, the tragic literary convention is defined differently according to whch particular scenarios are being examined. So it is that the classic interpretations of tragedy by Aristotle,[9] Nietzsche,[10] Hegel,[11] Unamuno,[12] and others each derive from concern with emphasizing one or another of the remaining 32 Greek tragedies. Their interpretations and analyses differ partly in terms of the chosen drama. Because of the literary convention of tragedy is a cultural phenomenon, it does *not* describe a dependable, invariant set of events. It may even be that any such term ("tragedy," the "Renaissance," literary realism, the "Aquarian age") is not more than a conceptual hedge, an illusion of order which we use to fend off total lunatic helplessness in the face of this overwhelmingly unordered life.

Surely my own perspective is also a biased, limited view, at least as misleading as it may be enlightening. Accepting this inevitable limitation, I will not fight against what must be but will try to give myself over to it openly and with gusto. So instead of trying to convince you of the unlimited value of what I have to say, I will attempt to caution you (and to disarm myself) by making my biases as transparent as I can.

I set out to write this book for many reasons. One of the fun reasons is my usual wish to get paid for opening myself to a new sort of pleasure. I get to pursue activities which my own inertia might have otherwise precluded my experiencing. In this area for instance, I have many cop-outs. I say to myself that though I love theater, it's often too much trouble to bother to get tickets. I somehow don't get around to getting hold of the plays I promise myself I'll read. Those slim volumes are over-priced and I often forget to return library books until they are long overdue.

Instead I set myself up to write a book on psychotherapy and theater. In this way, right off I create the constructive distraction of appearing to gear myself to deepening my understanding of my work with patients. But beyond lie the more private rewards of simple self-indulgence. I now find myself seeing and reading many plays I would have otherwise missed. I further enrich my understanding of these delights by sampling a wide range of related writings: the history of theater, the meaning of dramatic genres, critical evaluations of many plays, performances, and playwrights, I talk with actors, attend rehearsals when I can, and go off to theater workshops. A dormant aspect of my self comes to life. Again I have tricked myself into becoming more alive, and I love it.

I began by reading philosophical, historical, and aesthetic approaches to Tragedy. Where I could I sampled what actors, directors, and critics had to say about them. Then on to the plays. Determined to restore that discipline of mind which clears my inner vision I set out to read (or reread) every one of thirty-two surviving Greek Tragedies of Aeschylus, Sophocles, and Euripides, as well as commentaries on each. Once again I was sweeping out the cobwebs of a dusty mind from the corners of my half-closed eyes.

It worked again. It always works. And yet I always somehow forget, and let some of myself become clouded by unneeded disuse once more. Correcting this perennial temptation to mental lethargy is a little like taking on regular morning calesthenics, or daily periods of meditation, or ritual prayer. Just as body and spirit need regular awakening and restoring, so too does the mind. And like the others, when kept in condition this aspect of Self returns rewards far greater than the efforts reluctantly put into priming it.

And so it was that I came to read the plays, some for the first time, others in a new light. I saw performances where I could (more often having to settle for listening to recordings of performances). Of all these plays, one drew me back again and again, perhaps because to me it seems the most representative of the tragic tradition—because it has moved me repeatedly as theater, because the protagonists seem caught in struggles most reminiscent of what my patients endure, because these struggles are so like my own needless suffering. The play I speak of is *Antigone*,[13] the last of the Oedipus Trilogy which make up Sophocles' Theban plays, written and first performed in the city-state of ancient Athens almost 2500 years ago.

Antigone is, of course, one of the daughters of ill-famed Oedipus, he who unwittingly slew his own father (Laius) and married his own mother (Jocasta). He tried to flee from a prophecy that these misfortunes would occur, only to find that by his very efforts to escape, he brought about the actualization of those dark forebodings. Stubbornness and pridful insistence demanded that he disclose the entire catastrophe to his unbelieving eyes.

In despair, Jocasta hung herself, while Oedipus blinded himself and asked to be banished. Antigone accompanied her father into exile. But even when she returned to Thebes after his death, her troubles were far from over. Antigone's brothers were set against one another in a terrible struggle for royal power. Eteocles held the throne and had reneged on his promise to alternate his place in this highest seat with his brother, Polynices. In an attempt to seize that pivotal position, Polynices and his Argive allied armies led by seven Champions lay seige to the Seven Gates of Thebes. After a long and bloody battle, it was decided that the matter be settled in a single armed combat, a winner-take-all struggle between brother and brother. In this encounter, the sons of Oedipus killed one another. Polynices' invading hordes fled, and Jocasta's brother Creon became the new King of Thebes.

Creon respects dead Eteocles as defender of his city, and so believes he should be so honored. Polynices, on the other hand, has assaulted his own homeland. Whatever his personal motives, Creon views the dead man's actions as traitorous, and therefore deserving of Justice so that others will be encouraged to do what is right.

He orders the body of Eteocles be buried with honors, while issuing an edict that Polynices' body "be left unburied, unwept, a feast of flesh for keen-eyed carrion birds."[14] Anyone who should defy his order is to be stoned to death.

Antigone, whose love and family loyalty once led her to accompany her blind and banished father into exile, now finds that she continues to love her dead brother, whatever his politics. And so, as the play begins, she is asking her sister, Ismene, to help bury their brother, Polynices, though it is against Creon's order. But Ismene does not dare to join her sister in defying the law. Antigone will not be dissuaded by the threat of inevitable punishment.

Soon she is speaking to her sister with contempt. She speaks as the voice of Love, family loyalty, and natural law, setting herself over against Creon who speaks for Reason, political justice, and the gods of the State. By putting family above country (and heroism above helplessness), she has set in motion inevitably destructive forces. She is headed toward dramatic confrontation with Creon. An apparently irresistible force is about to meet a seemingly immovable object.

Willfully, she glamourizes her unyielding self-dramatization, saying to Ismene:

Go your own way; I will bury my brother;
And if I die for it, what happiness!
Convicted of reverence—I shall be content
To lie beside a brother whom I love.[15]

Hardly has Creon taken his own overstated stand, when a frightened, out-of-breath sentry arrives. He reluctantly reports that someone has already dared to defy the king by scattering "dry dust over the body . . . in the manner of holy burial."[16] Outraged Creon is quick to blame unknown citizens who disobeyed for a price or simply because they were rebellious. He ignores the cautioning voices of the Chorus. They speak with the outlook of ordinary non-heroic (and therefore, non-tragic) men, telling him he may be mistaken in his stubborn decree. The overthrow of his edict might "prove to be an act of the gods."[17] They warn that:

> . . . he that, (is) too rashly daring, walks in sin
> In solitary pride to his life's end.[18]

The sentry returns with his captive, Antigone, whom he has discovered in the act of burying her brother with her own hands. Creon tries to let her off the hook by suggestig that perhaps she was unaware that she was breaking the law and would be punished. Antigone says flatly that she knew clearly that he had forbidden anyone to bury Polynices. Arrogantly she goes on to tell King Creon:

> I did not think your edicts strong enough
> To overrule the unwritten unalterable laws
> Of God and heaven, you being only a man.[19]

She is glad to die. It is he who is foolish. The Chorus warns that she shows her father's stubborn spirit. She too has never learned to yield. Creon answers with the moral tone of tragedy. He warns her that:

> . . . The over-obstinate spirit
> is soonest broken; as the strongest iron will snap
> If over-tempered in the fire to brittleness.[20]

Glorying, martyr-like in her honorable crime, Antigone's willfulness increases. It grows exactly in proportion to her helplessness before the jeopardy in which she has put herself. The worse her situation becomes, the more spitefully she digs in.

Suspecting Ismene of complicity, Creon summons her to share Antigone's punishment. Ismene would now be glad to share the blame. Antigone rejects her sister's offer, refusing to share the spotlight with her.

Ismene pleads for mercy for Antigone. She reminds Creon that Antigone was to be married to his son, Haemon. Creon stubbornly remains the authoritarian patriarch. He is totally committed to social and political order at whatever cost of caring feelings and personal relationships. He insists that the law is *immutable*, and so Antigone *must* be executed.

Haemon comes to his father. He wishes to be the deferentially obedient son, and yet is determined to plead for his beloved's life. He tries to convince his father that this trouble-making edict is unpopular with the citizenry. This simply increases Creon's anger and arrogance. It also reduces him to an attempt at a misogynous misalliance with his son expressed in his stubbornly posturing:

> *Better be beaten, if need be, by a man,*
> *Than let a woman get the better of us.* [21]

Haemon is exasperated by his father's insistent disregard for feelings. Trying to maintain his devotion to paternal authority, he urges respectable compromise. He points out that:

> *It is no weakness for the wisest man*
> *To learn when he is wrong, know when to yield.* [22]

But Creon responds by becoming even more the patriarch. He would not think of taking advice from his son, "a fellow of his age." [23] He is the King, responsible only to himself. The State belongs to him. He knows what is best for everyone. Haemon leaves in disgust telling his self-willed father:

> *You'd be an excellent king—on a desert island.* [24]

At this point everyone is stuck and miserable. It feels like the situations I encounter when an internecine family conflict pours over into my office for consultation. Each person is sure that things could be better, if only *someone else* in the family would give in and change. Each one wants me to make things better, to fix his broken world. My questioning his own part in making this mess, only heightens the righteous, self-willed entrenching of his role as the heroic figure. After all, his efforts to be especially good result in his being even more unappreciated. He may not be able to get his own way. At the very least, he is heroically committed to seeing to it that he will not yield to anyone else's demands.

It is just at this point in the play that Creon begins to falter (at least in tragic terms). Though he insists on going on with Antigone's execution, inexplicably he changes the method from stoning to entombment. This change reveals some beginning awareness of his own human fallibility. It is his subtle attempt to give Antigone another chance to discover the absurdity of her own stubborn pride. Perhaps she, too, may change her mind and give in. It is in this transformation that the plays begins to lose in tragic force and commitment to divine principles. Now it can begin to gain in humanity and appreciation of man's perennial temptation to foolishness.

If only one of the protagonists could bend, perhaps neither would have to break. But in the classic tragic mode such surrender is no more likely than in its contemporary neurotic parrallel. Mournfully the Chorus intones:

You are the victim of your own self-will. [25]

So it is that both Antigone and Creon behave as though they were invulnerable and infallible. These same fictions which protect them from overwhelming feelings of helplessness and uncertainty, also lead them to destruction.

Antigone suppresses any doubts she might have about her own responsibilities for her misfortunes. She projects reponsibility by invoking the excuse of being a part of the ill-fated dynasty of Oedipus' family. It is like a foreshadowing of the Twentieth Century Freudian legacy of the: "But I had an unhappy childhood" cop-out.

It is time for the entrance of Teiresias, the blind seer and therapist-in-residence. He appears to charge Creon with destructive willfulness. As consultant, he states:

> . . . news you shall have; and advice, if you can heed it. [26]
> . . . The blight that is upon us is your doing . . .
> Only a fool is governed by self-will. [27]

He warns:

> . . . Even now the avenging Furies,
> The hunters of Hell that follow and destroy,
> Are lying in wait for you, and will have their prey,
> When the evil you have worked for others falls on you. [28]

Wisely, at that point the seer does not stay to struggle with his king. He instructs by example by doing his best, giving in and letting go of that which he cannot control. Creon now sees the wisdom of relenting before it is too late. But it is not so easy to surrender, even to himself. He tells us what we all know, and yet must relearn again and again:

> It is hard to give way, and hard to stand and abide
> The coming of the curse. Both ways are hard. [29]

Exposed as finally unheroic, Creon surrenders. Hard as it is for him to admit the error of his ways, he reverses his willful decision. He hurries off to bury dishonored Polynices, and then to release Antigone. In accepting defeat and compromise, he yields to his human limitations. He tries tolerating his hurt pride and helplessness, rather than continue his heroic rush toward tragic destruction. The Chorus sings a song of praise for his putting the general wellbeing above his stubborn pride.

But, alas, he has yielded not too little, but too late. By the time Creon reaches Antigone's tomb she has hung herself.

To the last she has gone her own way and made her own laws. Arrogantly she has refused to live whatever of this imperfect life was yet left to her. If she could not have her own way, at least she could see to it that Creon did not get his way with her. In the end, Tragic heroism cannot be distinguished from common-place spitefulness. Who commits suicide without some crypto-comic sense of self-satisfaction and smug superiority?

In classic tragic tradition, one catastrophe follows on the next. This dramatic convention is as empirically unsupported as the domino theory of one catastrophe supposedly leading to another and another and another. This contemporary heroic policy position kept us in Vietnam for so many futile, bloody years. If we left all Asia would fall, and the rest of the world follow suit. We could not leave in peace, not *without honor*. Our tragic flaw of pride would not permit our accepting our helplessness, our error, the absurdity of our principles. We ignored the necessity of giving in and going home. Our leaders would not admit that we were unheroic and no better than anyone else in that dumb play.

In *Antigone*, the lesson is taught by Haemon's discovery that his bride-to-be has died of an out-of-hand temper tantrum. It turns out to be contagious as Haemon tries to murder his father with a sword. The old man, no longer committed to tragic heroism, is free to run away to safety. In a case of mistaken identity, Haemon is reduced to killing himself instead.

His mother is not to be outdone. She decides that it is all more than she can possibly bear, and so, of course, she kills herself.

Creon turns out to be the only one in the family with a sense of his own foolishness and with enough decency and humility to see that he had made a big mistake. Only pathetic Creon is left with the family legacy of guilt, grief, and helplessness. Poor Creon is the only one with insight, unselfish motivation, and a willingness to change. The only decent prospect for psychotherapy in the bunch is left a wailing wreck of a man. How I would have hoped he might be able to find good counsel, learn to laugh at himself, grieve his losses, and go on to make a new life for himself.

But no! As a sixth century B.C. Greek Tragedy, our play ends with chorus moralizing:

Of happiness the crown
And chiefest part
Is wisdom, and to hold
The gods in awe.
This is the law
That, seeing the stricken heart
Of pride brought down,
We learn when we are old.

EXEUNT[30]

The world of Greek Tragedy is a universe ordered by divine principles. Any time that divine and human purposes conflict, the gods will be supreme. The thrust toward this inevitable consequence is set about by some man or woman given over to heroic striving toward godliness. This gets expressed in his (or her) self-willed nature, overblown virtues, and excessive pride. A man sees himself as invulnerable, presumes himself to be most unquestionably right. Just then he is most subject to divine retaliation. The gods restore order by bringing about his tragic fall. He is sure to meet the catastrophic consequences of his prideful actions, the suffering which his inexorable fate holds in store.

The tragic hero must learn through this suffering. But all that there is for him to learn is that he must live a life of moderation. His ways must not challenge higher principles. His only protection from divine retribution is learning the humility of enduring suffering with dignity. He must come to accept the inevitability of the universal tragic moral law: the hero always gets what he wants—and he always pays the full price.

There is much to be learned from the Greek sense of man's insignificance. But their insistence that there is some higher order distresses me. They teach us something about just which attitudes bring needless unhappiness. But then they go on to insist that if only we try to be well-behaved children, that if we are good, then we may live some optimal existence in a balanced world run in accordance with the absolutely dependable principles of the wise and fair divine parents.

The contention that people often suffer as a consequence of taking themselves too seriously is played out again and again on the classic Greek stage by the tragic hero. It is also a central theme in the consultation room of the contemporary psychotherapist, a theme with variations demonstrated by the neurotic patients who show up there to seek his help.

Like Antigone and Creon, the neurotic is a person who has lost perspective, a driven creature whose actions contribute to his own needless unhappiness. The neurotic does not necessarily carry a tragic flaw of character. Yet, like the tragic hero, he suffers from an imbalance or excess of what otherwise might be virtuous, creative, worthwhile, or at least fun.

There are certain daemonic qualities which, at their best, add pleasure and productivity, verve and color to our lives. Out of hand, these same lovely aspects that can be otherwise so creative, turn out to be the most destructive forces as well. I speak of sexual longing, anger, pride, the craving for power—and the like. Human strengths/weaknesses such as these are daemonic in the same way as "any natural function which has the power to take over the whole person."[31] Both in the neurotic, and in the tragic hero, virtues become exaggerated extensions of what they started out to be. The patient and the player become grotesque caricatures of their own initially creative thrust.

In the play, *Antigone*, the two protagonists are exaggeratedly daemonic personalities on a collision course. The play is often interpreted as a sort of an allegory between religion and politics, between family ties and patriotism. This analysis can be deepened by invoking the Jungian concept of archetypes.[32]

Archetypes are inherited modes of psychic functioning which can be recognized in the recurring motifs to be found in man's myths and dreams, in every time and in every place.

> The familiar motifs which repeat themselves again and again in dreams and in myths include such primordial images as the original Creation, the Great Mother both as fruitful womb and as devouring destroyer, the Great Father as Lord of Heaven, wise old man, and as wrathful judge, and the

> Child as the link with the past. The insoluble mysteries of the relation of male and female, darkness and light, heaven and earth, the ground work of existence itself make themselves known again and again . . .[33]

through the expressions of the archetypes of the collective unconscious present in each of us.

If we do not develop self-awareness, sometimes, these dark powers seem to take over. This occurs as a kind of daemonic possession. Sometimes it goes so far that "people can live archetypal lives."[34] It is as though they were almost allegorical figures representing some idealized image or higher principle. All therapists are familiar with the moralistic obsessional neurotic who caricatures the ideal of duty, or the finicky compulsive whose actions both mock and honor the ideal of orderliness.

We find this with Antigone and Creon (at least up until that point at which he becomes aware of what he is up to and of its terrible consequences). They are not simply two people with different ideas or conflicting needs. Each is overwhelmed by archetypal forces which direct his every action, write his every line, mold his entire character. Soon they are no longer a particular man and a particular woman, arguing over opposing views of a particular situation. She becomes Woman and he, Man. Eros faces Logos. The Great Mother and the Great Father pit Feeling against Reason, Loyalty against Justice, and Conscience over against Authority. The reverence of the passionate heart has become dramatized into Antigone's service to the dark underworld gods of Earth. Creon elevates his obedience of the controlled mind to the carrying out of the divine order of Heaven.

The original Greek concept of the *daemonic* involved a kind of dangerous ecstasy, a divine madness, well-suited to such Dionysian theatrical celebrations. The possessed person moves from a momentary state of creative inspiration to a chronic headlong plunge into a life of self-willed, sutbborn archetypal immersion. That which begins as a mere fascinating dramatic highlight ends up defining the whole damn play from beginning to end.

Antigone's assertion of the principle of love begins by raising her beyond the line of least resistance. It starts by spotlighting the best of her humanity. But once she is consumed by the temptation to heroic grandeur, that same commitment to Love is then exaggerated to something more than human. Engulfingly, it nearly destroys her personal capacity to care for those around her. It leads her to deny the presence of love in other people.

Creon's initial interest in discovering what is fair is also willfully expanded into being dangerously more than simple human wish to do the right thing. It leads him toward becoming a tyrannically unjust archetypal personification of the dark force of Justice. At that point, he is fair to no one, least of all to himself.

Neurotic behavior has much of this bigger-than-life, ironically self-defeating quality. Not that anyone's life should entirely lack theatrical intensity or dramatic moments. But all the world is *not* a stage, and all the men and women are *not* merely players. Life is *not* tragic, except for the neurotic. And then it is bad theater.

Theatrical performances require and audience. They are not lived for their own sake alone. So too with neurosis.

Actions on a stage are all meant to be relevant to the plot. Every line is to reflect the character of the speaker. The audience must be entertained. No room for irrelevencies, repetitions, or possible boredom. But life is more random, redundant, and often more meaningless than a good play. Only for the neurotic is it as stylized, as overplayed, as tragically intense as a bad play. Surely the audience for whom any given neurotic performs will be bored unless they too have the option of participating in some reciprocal amateur production in which each can play a part. You can be in my play if I can be in yours.

But how much better I feel when I am *not* acting out some tragically heroic role. Often in recent years I am able to retain enough dramatic intensity to bring meaning to my life, to keep its performance vibrant and entertaining, without having to play out the same neurotic parts matinee and evening without end. How much freer I feel when I am able to move beyond the tragedy of stylized, overly-rehearsed actions. How much happier I am when I move beyond cliche situations supported by obviously phony props and back-drops.

More and more of the time now I realize that I need not follow certain traditional dramatic conventions. I can throw away prescribed scripts. In a world unordered by divine wisdom, I am free of parental direction, criticism, or applause. In such a world, any action is permitted.

Now consequences are somewhat predictable, and yet always uncertain. The only future that is sure is that I must face the consequences of my acts, whatever they may be. In any case, I am more likely to be rewarded or punished by *how* I perform, than by any good or bad reviews which others may offer.

It is an unheroic, absurdly ordinary universe, a random world without ultimate order. In such a world, no one need be type-cast, and all lines may be ad-libbed. What others might say does not serve as a cue-line for a prepared speech. I can become more curious about what might come next. At such times I am able to move beyond the tragedy of my neurotic miscastings. At such moments, I am able to move a living theater out into the streets of spontaneity.

Chapter II
Freedom to Improvise

How then are we to gain the freedom to improvise? First we must learn to give up our studied, well-scripted, often miscast, bigger-than-life, tragic roles. ~~Rub~~

The original tragic heroes of classic Greek theater were literally outsized representations of exaggeratedly more-than-human proportions, very special sorts of characters. Already inflatedly top-heavy in traditional padded robes, their natural height was grotesquely enlarged by ornamental head-dress (*Onkos*) and by the thick soles on their high boots (*Cothurni*). To the artificial magnificence of their high-soled boots was added face-masks which at the same time identified the characters portrayed and served as megaphones! Surely their style of performance was as high-flown as their costuming.

It is necessary to limit my own role as a therapist, with its comparable costuming, props, and manner of delivery. I once believed that:

> *I must acquire the absurd title of "doctor."*
> *It will not make me a hair the better*
> *but as time goes, no man can be counted learned*
> *unless he is styled "Doctor."*
> *I must put on the lion's skin.*
> *I have to fight with monsters and*
> *I must wear the dress of Hercules.*
> (Erasmus) [1]

How far I have moved from that pompous and pedantic posture is probably best illustrated by my guerilla theater encounter with an establishment attempt at recasting me in the traditional role. That particular improvisation took place several years ago.

The American Academy of Psychotherapists was holding one of its annual summer workshops at the University of Wisconsin under the direction of Dr. Carl Whitaker who served as that year's conference chairman. It turned out that in order to get us the lovely accommodations that he wanted at the university, Carl had to do some political wheeling and dealing with the faculty. First they had wanted to participate with us. The workshops are such a wild, untraditional experience of happenings and free-form theater that Carl wisely discouraged that plan.

He worked out a compromise in which he agreed to have one of the training analysts on the faculty address the workshop participants. The man turned out to be a very stuffy, pedantic, obsessionally traditional orthodox psychoanalyst. Here we had stopped our free-form carrying-on to sit as an audience in this already constricting situation, and the guy turns out to be a creep.

He evidently did not know that he was addressing a group of some of the most talented and original maverick therapists in the country. As his lecture topic he chose to discuss the elementals of counter-transference. He droned on and on making his way ponderously through the basic Freudian concepts of the dangers of the therapist projecting and acting out his own unresolved unconscious conflicts in his relationship with the patient. This man's solutions numbered just two: one, if a problem arises, the therapist should go back and see his own analyst to resolve it; and two, any feeling that the therapist has for his patient should be distrusted, especially any feeling of affection.

Some members of the audience looked irritated. The rest simply looked sleepy. I of course found myself in the forefront of the first group.

When I'd had about enough, I raised my hand. The lecturer did not understand that this meant that I wanted to leave the room. Instead he smiled patronizingly and told me that he would be glad to answer any question I might ask.

I rose noisily. The other members of the audience looked at me with expressions ranging from delight at the prospect of some interruption of the proceedings, to annoyance that I might simply prolong them.

Undaunted I spoke up with just the right combination of intense interest and polite constraint:

"Let's see if I've got this straight, doctor. Any personal feelings I might have toward my patients are residues of my own unconscious conflicts, right?"

Our leader nodded approvingly.

I went on: "And we must never naively assume that personal feelings for a patient are genuine and appropriate?"

Again: "Yes, yes. Quite so!"

Myself: "Then I have just one more question, doctor. Does all of this business about the dangers of countertransference mean I have to stop fucking my patients?"

The speaker was shocked, appalled. The audience broke up.

Since then I have had the advantage of further coaching in such disruptive open theater improvisations offered by the brief engagements of the liberated teen-agers of the sixties and seventies. Led by the Bread & Puppet and the San Francisco Mime Troupes they held their one-shot or random stagings of guerrilla theater in the streets and parks of New York and Washington. Challenging the over-stuffed immorality of the traditional cultural structure, they held anti-war vigils in front of Saint Patrick's Cathedral and anti-celebrations at a Counter-Inaugural in our nation's capital. Suffocating under the destructive direction of those who had tried to cast them in traditional set-pieces, they met this painful prescribed absurdity with a playful *proscribed* absurdity of their own. Wherever they struck, the kids insisted that "spontaneity by definition means a radical shift in control."[2]

Their social-political struggle arouses echoes in me of my own fight against personal miscasting so many years ago.

I was fourteen or fifteen years old, just past puberty, and feeling more manly than the family could tolerate. My mother seemed especially disturbed by any sign of sexual maturity or independence. She would say things like: "Just because you've got hair on your chest doesn't mean you're a big shot." But clearly it was not the hair on my chest which most distressed her. She finally opted for splitting the difference with me by displacing the location of the crisis to the hair which had begun to grow under my arms.

She insisted that a "Big horse like you" should begin to use underarm deodorants. Then she began to nag that these deodorants would not be effective unless I shaved the hair under my arms as she did under hers. I still feel embarrassed to remember that I was at that time so much cast within the family scenario that I somehow went along with this symbolic ritual castration. At some point when my father was "on the road" she "helped" me with this problem.

By the time my father returned I had managed to develop an infection under one arm. We assumed it was my somehow inadequate response to my mother's understandable accidentally nicking my armpit with the "safety razor" with which I had been emasculated.

Though I was not wise enough to protest to my father about what had gone on, I did complain about the discomfort caused by the infection. Or perhaps I was wise enough to sense in advance that I would have gotten no support from him in combatting my mother's assault. After all, his being "on the road" was itself his yielding to my mother's pressure that he prove himself a man by making more money. He was not the sort who would have protested that he was already a man and that no proof was needed. Demonstrating that he was a good husband and father by being away from his wife and child made no sense.

I asked my father if I could go to a doctor to get some relief from the increasingly painful heat and pressure which I was experiencing in my armpit. But he was too smart for them. He told me: "Doctors make money by getting you to come for needless consultations, for extra visits, for advice that you can give yourself."

He went one: "If I take you to the doctor he'll charge me $4, tell me to take you home and have you put hot wet compresses under your arm so that the infection can drain, and then he'll tell me to come back and pay another $4 next week so he can see that you are cured. I'll tell you what," he said. "I won't take you to the doctor. Instead I'll keep you home and I'll advise myself that you should have hot wet compresses and that will save me $4 and then next week after you use them I'll check under your arm and see that you're cured and that will save me another $4."

I protested weakly and without effect. I tried using the hot wet compresses for several days. The infection seemed to grow worse. I had trouble sleeping because of the pain. The area grew swollen and the angry redness spread on my body instead of within the family where it belonged. Within a few days it got so bad that I had to see a doctor.

For that $4 he merely told us that I had to go into a hospital immediately for minor emergency surgery on what had become a potentially dangerous compound abcess. It was my first return to the Royal Hospital since I had made the mistake of being born there. I was very scared but the surgery was simple and was soon over.

I stayed at the hospital overnight and by the next morning was released to go home. My father came to pick me up. He was silent until we hit the street. I felt hurt and angry but expected so little in the way of understanding that I too was silent.

Once on the street my father spoke. "That was really, really awful," he said with more feeling than I ever had remembered hearing from him before. I turned expectantly toward him, hoping that for once someone regretted what I had been put through. My father went on: "Really, really awful," he wailed. "Can you imagine that? That bastard-anesthesiologist charged me $25, twenty-five dollars just for putting you to sleep for a few minutes."

My father looked even more distressed and bewildered as he watched incredulously as I took out my wallet, pulled out the few dollar bills it contained, tore them into pieces and scattered them in the warm summer Bronx breeze. "They'll never do those things to me again. From now on I'm going to do things my own way." I swore silently as I hurried down the street by myself, crying and alone.

Sometimes we must experience pain to the limits of what we can endure before we are able to question what is appearance and what is reality. It is so easy to be tempted to remain stuck in a limited life role which offers little reward beyond its safe sense of familiarity. No matter how dangerous the consequences of staying in character, each of us is sometimes tempted to live out his tragic role, than risk a new part or an unfamiliar, who-knows-what-will-happen-next improvisation.

A patient of mine was stuck in this way, fearful of reaching for the freedom to improvise. Daughter of a drunken suicidal father and a saccharine, feeling-denying mother, Karen spent much of her adult life seeking to become the loved little girl she had missed being as a child. The price was exorbitant. She tried hard to please and when someone found her acceptable she felt high on the fantasy that she was a good little girl loved at last. But at those times when she could not arrange to be the object of someone else's approval she felt as desperately lost and alone as when she had growing up in that awful house so long ago.

After some experience in therapy, Karen could see that in order to leave the dreadful depression of being a lost little girl behind her, she would have to give up the ephemerel fantasied rush of being a loved little girl. She saw the choice but still she hesitated.

In order to illustrate the irony of her delimma, I told her of the classic piece of business which comedian Jack Benny made famous. Years ago on his radio show, there was an episode in which Mr. Benny was walking alone down a dark street. The radio audience knew that the stock-in-trade of his comic character was his studied miserliness. And so audience tension was high when Mr. Benny was confronted by a street maurader whose sullen voice demanded, "Your money or your life."

The demand was followed by Mr. Benny's silence.

Again the mugger insisted, the threatening harshness of his voice growing louder, "I said, 'Your money or your life!'"

Again, Benny's silence.

"For the last time," the mugger shouted. "Your money or your life!"

Another brief silence, and Mr. Benny whined, "I know, I know! (long pause) I'm thinking it over."

Even the most natural improvisations become unavailable in someone who has been oppressively miscast in an overly scripted life. Sometimes it is necessary to remind patients that there must have been some time in their life when they reached out when they felt loving, shouted when they felt angry, and cried when they hurt. Such people have come to feel so locked into prescribed roles that though they cannot deny that as very little children they must have once felt free to do as they pleased, they cannot remember ever having had that freedom. All they know now is that it is forbidden to improvise.

Arthur Schopenhauer recounts a theater story which captures the flavor of such cruelly stilted direction. He tells:

> . . . of an actor, called Unzelmann, who was rebuked by his director and colleagues for too much improvising. One day Unzelmann appeared in a play that demanded his presence on stage with a horse. During the performance the horse dropped something natural to the horse, but unbecoming and unusual in the midst of a scene. The audience roared with laughter. Unzelmann turned to the horse and said: "Don't you know we are forbidden to improvise?"[3]

Even when people realize that they are allowed to change and to do as they please, they may be afraid that they will not be able to handle new situations. Psychotherapy patients like the rest of us are of course understandably reluctant to give up roles in which they feel competent and confident for the uncertainty of future improvisation.

When a patient is struggling with such a problem, I sometimes tell him the story about my son Nick's feelings of dread as he anticipated sixth-grade mathematics.

He was in fourth-grade at the time, his next oldest brother in sixth-grade. Nick was listening to David talk about his own work in that term's sixth-grade math. Nick commented uncomfortably: "I'll never be able to do that kind of homework."

I assured him that he certainly would be able to do it when the time came. Nick's poignant response was, "Don't be silly, Dad. How could a fourth-grader handle sixth-grade math?"

The therapist must be careful not to help too much when the patient is anticipating his own handling of sixth-grade math. He must remember the story of the boy who out of compassion tried to help free an emerging butterfly from his sticky cocoon. The butterfly got out but immediately fell helplessly to the ground unable to fly. Fortunately, the boy's father was there to explain that the struggle to emerge from the sticky cocoon is precisely what is needed to strengthen the butterfly's wings enough for him to be able to fly once he is free. The boy then understood that in doing the butterfly this favor, he had done him no favor.

Even when we feel able to cope with new ventures, our vision of ourselves in relation to our audience may lead us to resist going on to new ways of acting. How often we all struggle against improvising new roles even when it is clearly to everyone's advantage that we do so. The changing roles invited by the Women's Liberation Movement offer many poignant examples, some funny, some sad, some a bit of each. A peculiar instance arose recently in the North Carolina State Legislature in which the Equal Rights Amendment was defeated. It had been passed one day by preliminary vote only to be defeated the next in the final tally by two last minute vote switches:

> One changed vote was that of a woman, Representative
> Myrtle E. (Lulu Belle) Wiseman, who tearfully explained
> later that her switch was caused by a flood of phone
> calls from friends and neighbors back home in Avery
> County.
> "I know they don't know what E.R.A. is all about,"
> Mrs. Wiseman was quoted as having said to all the press
> services, "But I just couldn't in my own heart vote
> against my people."[4]

So she voted against herself instead.

There may be helpers along the way, but other people's expectations often turn out to be more of a hindrance than a help. In the long run, the freedom to improvise often requires that we give up hope of having an appreciative audience. Too often the onlookers are too ready to ask that we do it some other way than our own, that not our will, but theirs be done. I've seen friends get their things together, change "serious" roles for the fun of improvising only to be met with criticism instead of pleasurable appreciation that their new happiness might understandably inspire. That's how it was for Salik.

It was during one summer vacation on Cape Cod that I first met Salik. For years he had been a very successful practicing psychoanalyst in New York City. It was on a vacation of his own that he found the freeing experiences which ultimately allowed him to give up the studied role which his middle European Jewish culture had dictated, to take on a scary but exciting life of daily improvisation. Salik had gone go Haiti for just three weeks. There he met a beautiful black butterfly of a woman, a Haitian actress and primitive painter.

Salik himself had long loved to paint. But his official role necessitated his reducing this first love to nothing more than a hobby.

By the time the end jof the Haitian vacation grew near they knew that they loved each other. For a few days they played at plans about how they would get together again in the future. But at last Salik realized that this was empty fantasy. If he left her now, that would be the end of it.

Instead they decided to marry then and there. His wife returned to New York with him to help him close down his practice, to gather up what little money they both had, and to move toward redefining their own lives in terms of doing the painting that was most important to each of them. They tried to figure out how long they could live on the little money they had and the bit more they expected to make. Salik told me that their working plan was to count on spending $4,000 a year for necessities, and another $4,000 for incidentals.

By the time I met them they had been married for several years, and had three strangely beautiful children. They were living six months out of the year in a house on Gull Pond on the Cape, and the other six months in Cuernavaca, Mexico. When I asked how difficult it was for the children to have to shift back and forth between living in an English-speaking country and then in a Spanish-speaking country, and then back again, they laughed. It turned out that they all spoke French at home and just kind of adlibbed in whatever community they found themselves.

Salik himself had become a satisfyingly successful colorist painter after a while. That summer Marjorie and I bought from him a large canvas in powerful intensities of dark mottled yellows and astonishing floods of red.

As we got to know each other Salik told me of the confusion in the audience that came as he switched roles. After being away from New York for a while, his painting began to get some recognition. His agent told him that a one-man show of his work was being arranged in New York. He went back there for the first time in many many months to help work out the show into being all that he had hoped for.

He contacted some of his old psychoanalyst friends. They were delighted to hear from him and arranged a party. Showing great pleasure in welcoming him back they all offered to help him to open a new practice and to restore him to his true role.

Salik was grateful but assured them that he was happy and successful as an artist. The party broke up early. None of the other analysts ever called him again. Finally, he realized that they had only been happy to see him because, mistakenly, they were sure he was returning because he had failed.

Salik's story was recently brought to mind again by the improvisation of another friend. Gary is the president of a social-problem-solving company. Recently he has discovered quite another sort of pleasure in his life. Gary has begun baking many wonderful loaves of bread. He loves the working with the dough, the baking, the hot sweet-smelling loaves, the eating of it, and the giving of it to his friends. He has begun to take off two or three afternoons a week from his role as president of the company in order to stay at home and bake.

Someone from out of his past was in town for a conference. She called Gary, visited him and his wife, and enquired with interest about all of his latest accomplishments. When he spoke in the moving way that he does of his new found delight in being a baker, she wasn't sure exactly how to respond. Unfortunately, she recovered her poise by replying that that was really wonderful for Gary because his descriptions of the esthetic and sensual pleasure of kneading the dough made it clear to her that he was on his way to becoming a sculptor!

We must learn to maintain a freedom to improvise parts for ourselves guided by inner wishes and to our own pleasure, rather than by what our audiences have in mind. Another friend helped make me even more clearly aware of this struggle.

Toby is a jazz pianist, composer, and music teacher, who comes from an Ivy-league accomplishment-oriented family. This made for some family resistance when as a teenager he chose to go to a music conservatory instead of a "real" college. Even if he had chosen a traditional academic route, in describing their children his parents surely would have said that one of their sons goes to Princeton and the other just goes to college.

Toby gave himself to studies at the conservatory as fully as he gives himself to anything else that intrigues him. Being Toby, when he had learned as much as he thought the conservatory had to teach him, he of course left to go on to work things out for himself. It was years later that he learned that his family had considered this move from the formal role of music student (which they had begun to accept) to that of improvising musician, was judged by them to be a mark of his failure as a dropout.

As a youngster and teenager, all of my own efforts to improvise were looked upon with disfavor. Nonetheless, once having begun to break loose I tried many things. Some turned out well. Some turned out badly. But the trying was as always exciting. Ever since I tried the worst I tried was good.

I remember particularly my own interest in music. Many of the teenagers with whom I hung around were practicing musicians. My own family had urged me to study piano, like my good cousins did. I had seen them pushed to perform like household pets or performing seals. Much to my parents' dismay I would rather be at liberty than audition for a trained animal act.

I did however, by the time I was sixteen, develop an interest in playing the guitar. I was working after school at the time. On my own I saved some money, went down to the Musican exchange and bought a second-hand guitar for $18. I sought out a teacher and made arrangements for lessons. I studied for six months.

Though I never became a fine guitarist in career terms, I did have fun. Beyond that, my brief adventure with the guitar has resulted in a lifelong deepening of my appreciation of the music to which I listen.

At the end of six months I had had enough. I terminated my lessons and resold my guitar for exactly $18, the original price. I was delighted.

It was a shock to me when later, during one of their critical reviews my parents said to me: "Everything you try and everything you fail at. Just like you failed with the guitar."

As a performing art, music has always seemed particularly instructive to me as a model for what a freely improvised life can be like. I remember reading one musician's description of his giving up playing the recorder to go on to learn to play the flute. On the first instrument he had played competently in a well-trained but timid style. Going on to the flute was frightening but opened him to a new freedom of improvisation. Here is how he described the experience:

> Wandering over the unfamiliar terrain of a new instrument, my fingers broke free of their recorder habits, to new rhythms and patterns, reflecting what I'd heard but born from the moment. I could wave them *freely*—not always, but enough at times to express what was in me. Sometimes still, jamming with others, when I am down or ill at ease, I can hear myself "going through the motions," appearing to make music in a whole when actually my mind is checking off the chord changes and dragging familiar licks out of storage for my fingers to permute. But if we start cooking together, I can feel almost a click in me as another *system* takes hold in response, and energy flows from within through my fingers, which leap their baroquish walls to skitter across the keys, chasing the wind.[5]

He goes on to explore the experience of allowing himself this freedom:

> What are the traps? If I am anxious for the next note, or about it, I do not listen to the one I am in. *Be where I am.* If I am anxious to hang on to the goodness of where I am, for fear any change may make the note more sour, my body translates this into frozen fingers and lips that cannot move. *Don't be afraid to let go; learn to have nothng to lose.* To move in holy indifference is not to be passive . . . [6]

Yet sometimes the music itself leads me forth, embracing even my tremors and contradictions in something whole. Playing free, every so often I realize that the note I have just begun is not the one "I" had intended and sent out orders to produce, but a different one chosen confidently by my body to extend the music—quite independently of the listening-and-scheming me who flashes with resentment at the *mistake*. [7]

My instruction by this man was expanded by another highly creative musician. Toby and I had gone together to see the Bill Evans Trio perform at a Smithsonian Institution Jazz Concert. Evans is a player and composer who has re-harmonized the piano for a generation of jazz players. The trio consists of himself, a bass player, and a drummer. Unlike most other such trios these men seem in many ways equally matched. In most numbers the other players are featured for solo performances rather than merely serving as a setting for his piano playing. The bassist, Eddie Gomez, performed remarkably lyrical improvisations in his seemingly unlikely instrument. The bass is usually the equivalent in some ways to the Oriental drone, offering persistent background rhythm and not much in the way of melody or ideas.

The drummer, Marty Morrell, is best described by Bill Evans himself, when he says, "If Marty were playing with a feather there would still be fire in his touch."

Before the evening concert, there was a jazz workshop in the afternoon. The trio offered a brief informal concert and then left themselves open to questions from the audience. This is an extremely hazardous thing to do in that it seems to invite a great deal of ego-tripping, and expression of resentment born of envy, when the otherwise adoring audience is given a chance to switch itself into performance roles.

Nonetheless, Evans fielded the questions with grace, poise, and intelligence. His low-keyed, slow-moving subtle wit was not an easy target for the barbs which he encountered.

Question: "In what direction are you headed musically, Mr. Evans?" Answer: "(long thoughtful pause) What direction am I headed in? I would say . . . *down* . . . and, of course, . . . *in!*"

Evans then goes on to explain something about deepening his sense of what he is doing. He has always followed his own direction rather than collective trends. He works hard to master some mode of music, some working of the chords. He works, and works, and works, and works, until finally that aspect of the music is available to him "at an unconscious level."

But her warns that once you get something that well in hand then you have to be very careful not to become lazy and fall into it rather than take each new moment of music and do something immediate in response to it.

At that point someone else asked him "How often do you work out in advance any improvisation you may play within a given performance?"

Evans' answer was, unhesitating: "Never!"

Another question: "I've been a musician for twenty years but I still can't improvise. How do I get a feeling for jazz?"

Evans' answer: "Practice!"

Freedom to improvise requires a radical shift from familiar patterns, risking the displeasure and discouragement of the audience. It means giving up familiar pain for the pain of the unfamiliar. Sometimes it requires being able to laugh at ourselves and enduring the ridicule of others. Often it requires hard work. Other times it demands that we give up working hard so that we may begin to play. At many junctures it's hard to know which direction to take. For some of us, at some times in our lives, it is not possible to free ourselves without having someone we can count on to stand by and help, someone who cares about us but not about how we choose to live. Having someone to help me made the difference between tragic terror the first time I went crazy and comic relief the second time.

I have described in detail in my earlier writings the horror of my first psychotic episode.[8] Following and in part precipitated by undergoing my first bout of brain surgery, that experience was infused with left-over fragments of unresolved emotional turmoil, unrelated to the surgery itself. My delusion of being in hell, the victim of strange impersonal powers which would humiliate, torture, and even kill me, was a reconfiguration of the anguished helplessness of my growing up as a child who was to be indicted for all of the evil which my parents found it too hard to endure in themselves.

Between that episode and the next, during those confusing years in which I learned to come to live more acceptingly with my distress, my physical pain, and my foreshortened life, I returned to psychotherapy as a patient once more. Three times a week for almost two years I immersed myself once more in the guided soul-searching which allowed me to come to learn to better accept my life as it is, complain as I need to, and enjoy what I can. One of the unexpected benefits of these explorations came in the form of a more benign (if inevitable) second psychotic episode following my next surgical encounter.

Again my confusion began in the recovery-room following twelve hours of intra-cranial surgery. The most striking immediate subjective result of this surgical assault on my brain-stem was a catastrophically traumatic (temporary) shift in my visual and kinesthetic orientation. I woke to find myself flat on my back, plugged into various intravenous leads into my arms, and uncertain at first of where I was. I figured out in what seemed rather short order that I had just come out of surgery and was under intensive care in the recovery room. However, the surgical intervention had struck at some pivot of spatial orientation in my mind so that perceptually, the vertical and horizontal aspects of my world were reversed. Of course I could *not* know at the time that this was what was happening. All I could tell was that I seemed to be tied to a bed that stood upright, fearful that I would fall forward and crash against what looked like a wall that stood where the floor should have been.

I find it difficult to write of this experience because simply recalling it induces vertigo and a fear of toppling over. It was also confusing to see the white uniformed nurses and attendants seeming to glide by me perpendicularly as if they moved smoothly and gradually from the floor to the ceiling or from the ceiling to the floor.

My vision was also impaired in a peculiar way. The motleyed patterns on the surface of walls seemed to be continually moving in unpredicatably swirling configurations.

The combined results of my distorted sense of spatial

orientation and the unpredictable variations in my visual perceptions at first confused me. But though it all made no sense to me, I was not so much anxious as puzzled and intrigued. I cannot now reconstruct exact time sequences for that period, but in retrospect it seems that pretty soon I had developed a way of recreating this contradictory world into something I could enjoy. It was several days later before I recognized that this improvisation which served to settle my temporary cognitive dissonance was in fact a benign delusion.

At the time, I simply discovered that I was in a funhouse. It reminded me of the antic-modern neighbors' home across the road from my own, one in which I had watched their imaginatively zany teen-age kids grow up.

So it was that I combined my memory traces of their children's involvements in music, the physical and natural sciences, and the freak drug-culture, as I created a new play-space for them. The recovery room became a psychedelic recreational basement complete with swirling lights, gently swarming butterflies, and twisting-turning, gravity-defying architecture in which people could walk on walls and pass each other in fourth dimensional space.

I was paranoid enough to be cunning about all of this. When a nurse or doctor would check to see whether or not I was disoriented, I would tell them just exactly who and where I was, leavng out only the fact that I knew that this was a funhouse. They tried to fool me, but it was I who fooled them. Once it was all over, the only aspect of this that disturbed me was that I had fooled my wife, Marjorie, as well. I was sure that once back in my own hospital room that I had told her that I saw insects swarming on her coat. From her point of view, I had not said anything to indicate that I was psychotic at the time.

Some things I'll never get straight. Enough that with my therapist's help I was allowed during this crazy time to be free of old miscastings, so that even unconsciously I could improvise a good trip.

If I must give up my place in some other people's worlds to live life as I choose, I put aside the old roles without regret. I will find what I need within my own freedom. The good will of others on their own trips will be enough to sustain me, just as they may be nurtured by my respect for their freedom to improvise. *Ruб*

We must learn that there are some limits to our ability to improvise. How I deal with limitations of my illness, the pain and the fatigue, is a matter of style and ad-libbing. However, there is no way that I can change my situation which would completely eliminate either of these burdens. It would not work any better than the decision of that black man who determined that he had overcome his racial hangups by deciding to convert!

Yet I would go to the edge before I discover that point at which I must turn back. Doing things my own way doesn't make the world into just what I'd like it to be, but that free style does turn out to be a hell of an exciting trip.

And even if I do give up old roles, get beyond old problems, some of my new routines might be as hokey as my old ones. I have spent so much time fooling other people, I sometimes can end up fooling myself. The dangers are perhaps particularly great in the current setting of our counter-cultural, encounter group, mystical-occult, Aquarian Age where there are ready-made mass-media modelled costumes, props, and lines for the new free spirits, for those of us who would be the contemporary improvisers. Recently I came across a delightful Zen-on-Zen story, a helpful cautionary reminder for guarding against my own predilection for such stereotyped stylish solutions.

Traditionally Zen monasteries will only admit wandering Zen monks if they can show proof of having solved a *koan*.

It seems that a monk once knocked on a monastery gate. The monk who opened the gate didn't say 'Hello' or 'Good morning,' but 'Show me your original face, the face you had before your father and mother were born.' The monk who wanted a room for the night smiled, pulled a sandle off his foot and hit his questioner in the face with it. The other monk stepped back, bowed respectfully and bade the visitor welcome. After dinner host and guest started a conversation, and the host complimented his guest on his splendid answer.

'Do you yourself know the answer to the *koan* you gave me?' the guest asked.

'No,' answered the host, 'but I knew that your answer was right. You didn't hesitate for a moment. It came out quite spontaneously. It agreed exactly with everything I have ever heard or read about Zen.'

The guest didn't say anything, and sipped his tea. Suddenly the host became suspicious. There was something in the face of his guest which he didn't like.

'You *do* know the answer, don't you?' he asked.

The guest began to laugh and finally rolled over on the mat with mirth.

'No,' reverend brother,' he said, 'but I too have read a lot and heard a lot about Zen.' [9]

As a working psychotherapist, I too have read a lot and heard a lot about Zen. In my field the equivalent areas of study are Freud, Jung, Gestalt, Non-Directive Therapy, and the like. In each lies the danger of the therapist seeming to be enlightened when he has done no more than take on the semblance of one of these new roles or orientations, the semblance without the substance. Too often technical jargon is offered as a substitute for real understanding of what the therapist is about. He may be so caught up in his own self-importance as a star that he learns to take on the appearance of doing the work in a particular orientation without a full immersion in the part in which he has cast himself. Staislavski would have warned him:

Love the art in yourself, not yourself in the art.[10]

First it is necessary for a therapist to learn his part in depth in a disciplined manner. Only then can he be free to improvise with full confidence that he knows his part well enough to trust that his ad-libbing will be authentically creative and not just a flurry of irresponsible throw-away lines.

. . . moments of "subconsious" creative (occur)
when an actor *improvises* . . . (only when) his text
and the pattern of his role are firmly fixed . . . [11]

(because) There are no accidents in art—only the
fruits of long labor.[12]

One danger is that the therapist may *not* commit himself fully enough to his role to improvise freely, that he may *not* immerse himself deeply enough in a particular tradition to be able to break with that tradition in truly creative ways.

The opposite is also true. Very young therapists (and very old ones) are in the greatest danger of succumbing to the temptation of finding *the one true way*, that known and trust path which will supply a fool-proof secnario for dealing with any unexpected situation in the same stilted manner.

So it is that the very young "discover" the answer. Barely having begun the search, they already become orthodox Primal Therapists, Bio-Energeticists, or some other devotee of the Guru-of-the-Month Club.

Older therapists like myself my be tempted to feel that they have "invented" the one true way. I remember the chilling experience of asking someone who had come to study with me what he wanted to learn. He answered: "I want to become a Koppian therapist." Shocked I replied: "My God, for years I've been trying to avoid becoming one myself."

In order to guard against such an oppressive restriction of my own freedom to improvise, I must remind myself to be responsive to each patient at each moment as free of cliche performing tricks as I can be. This requires learning many parts well and then giving them all up except as they are called forth in a new and fresh form by what is going on with a particular patient at a particular time. Perhaps this aspect of improvisation will be clearer if I describe a "typical" segment of my work with patients.

This morning was as typically variegated as most. My work consisted in seeing four patients, all of whom were women. That, in itself, was somewhat typical because in our culture women have more support than men for seeking help from others, for talk, exploration, and relationship rather than action as the basis for getting help. Men are the last to seek therapy, and the first to give it up during an economic crisis. Furthermore, because of the cultural structure, I tend to see women more often earlier in the day when their children are at school, and men later in the day at the end of their workday stint or during a late lunch hour break from their daily chores.

The first patient came in with a dream which spoke of her conflict between her own sexual longings and the inhibiting, critical, moralistic aspects of herself. Ideally, she would like to be sexually aware, responsive, and even initiatory with her husband. Instead, she finds herself "frigid," resentful, and self-depreciating. Most of the work that hour consisted in my encouraging a Gestalt dialogue between the idealized, sexually free, oppressed or victimized part of herself on the one hand and the "crumby" moralistic, persecutory, bad-mother part of herself. Alternately taking on the timid, whiney voice of the victim on the other hand, and the stridently superior and critical voice of the persecutor on the other, she engaged in a struggle between the exchange, she found that she did not have to fight the battle to death but could grow in stature and independence, turn on her heel and walk away freely from the persecutory part of herself. She left the hour feeling more confident and stronger about her right to her own sexual freedom.

The second patient discussed her marriage in terms of her movement away from jealousy about her husband's wanting to go places on his own, in terms of taking a night out for herself. While she felt freed from her preoccupation with her jealousy of what he was up to, she felt conflicted about her right to have a life of her own, and her temptation to violate the marriage in the process. In this case I worked with the patient by comparing her marital struggles with my own and encouraging a dialogue between her and myself in the context of the man-woman problems with which we all must deal. We both found this supportive, horrifying, and (hopefully) promising better solutions in each of our marriages.

Patient number three came in feeling very good about herself in relation to work we had done in the past and some things that she had gotten together for herself during the week. Some anxiety was expressed and we worked on a relationship level around her difficulty in finding herself sufficient without being critical of herself as her mother had been. She then related her dreams and some preoccupations about death and concentration camp images, and the Anne Frank diaries. I responded by encouraging the psychoanalytic work of free association and of linking her childhood to the concentration camp images. She made some progress on sorting out the part of her response to the holocaust as being that of any sensitive human. Then she went on to that part of these preoccupations which serve as residual symbolic expressions of unresolve childhood conflict.

Patient number four came in enmeshed in the previous few days' maritan conflicts. With her I explored the problems in terms of Jungian psychological types, helping her to identify where she was in the conflict simply on the basis of who she was and what her basic attitudes are, and how they conflicted with her husband's cognitive style and his basic psychological type. This seemed to help support in her the confidence that some of the conflicts could be resolved without either one of them having to be changed or be done in.

Four different patients, four different styles of therapeutic approach on my part, four different sorts of personal experiences. In such a typical morning's work, one need only learn to expect the unexpected, and to be free to improvise.

Later that same day I spent an hour with a young couple whom I had been seeing in conjoint therapy for marital difficultires. As they worked through some of their troubles, their sexual relations had temporarily improved. They had expressed pleasure about this change, but it was clear that they found it somewhat unsettling.

It was soon therafter that they came in to see me on that particular afternoon. clearly the young man was very upset. He said, "You've got to help me, doc. For the past two weeks my wife has had trouble having an orgasm. I know that if I loved her enough and I was enough of a man I could satisfy her. Tell me, what am I doing wrong?"

I told him that I didn't know why he was more upset about *her* problem than she was. However, if he insisted that his happiness depended upon getting his wife to have an orgasm, certainly I would try to help them.

I asked her how she experienced all this since she seemed hardly perturbed. She replied, "I just can't help it. Every time we've made love for two weeks now, just when I begin to get excited, a song runs through my mind and distracts me, and so you see, at a time like that I just can't have an orgasm." I told her I understood and could see how that could separate her from her own feelings and separate them in the process, but that I knew just how to solve the problem. They both expressed an uneasy enthusiasm about the possibility of an immediate solution.

I questioned her, asking if the melody was always the same. She answered yes, it was an old familiar song.

Interrupting my dialogue with the young woman I turned to her husband and demanded, "Can you sing?" He said, "Oh, sure, but what has that got to do with it?"

I sugested that the tension between them could be resolve if she would tell him just what song it is that keeps running through her mind. She was to do so before the next time they chose to make love. But I pointed out that the problem could only be resolved if, during the lovemaking, when a song began to run through her mind, she would signal him that that was going on. At that point, I instructed him, he was to join her in a duet.

When they returned for their therapy session the following week they were ready to talk about other more threatening problems in the relationship. They had begun to follow my instructions in the bedroom during the preceding week, but found that they got to laughing and fooling around so much that his adequacy and her orgasm were no longer a focus of their attention. They had somehow ended up just having a great deal of fun together in bed.

Chapter III
Before the Final Curtain

I set out to write this book aware only of my fascination with theater, of the power of that metaphor in my work as a psychotherapist, and of the continuing inner sense that I have no choice but to go on writing. From the outset, I had no question but that the working title of this outpouring had to be *Beyond Tragedy*. Guided once more by the knowing hand of my unconscious dreaming self, I was well into the manuscript before I realized that I was once more going on with the work on my Self, that the title named the psychological space into which I was heading, that I was once again writing to instruct myself as to what I must become in my life.

Once more, circumstances conspired to show me the way. This time the denouement came in the form of a "mistake" in timing. I had written a piece titled, "Teach Your Children Well." It appears earlier in this book as the segment in which my son, Jon, and I talk about how each of us feels about the fact that I don't have very long to live.[1]

I had timed its separate publication[2] to follow the appearance of my last book, *The Hanged Man*.[3] In that book, I describe in some detail my second ordeal of neurosurgery, the current state of my health, and the implications for what life I have left. Publication of that book was delayed by some months, and I insisted on ignoring the effects this delay would have on the impact of "Teach Your Children Well."

The article appeared in *Pilgrimage*, a journal of pastoral psychotherapy. As usual, I sent out reprints of the piece to people on my mailing list: to friends, to certain members of the psychotherapeutic community, and to generous strangers who have responded to my books by writing to me.

Soon I received a flood of responsive letters and phone calls from people who cared and whom I had unwittingly caught off-guard. I was filled with regret at having subjected them to the needless pain of having to learn of my situation in such a seemingly off-handed way. I wrote and spoke to each of them about how sorry I was to have pained them so, and of how moved I was by their concern.

In order to tell them just where I stood with regard to my own situation, I was forced to improvise the stand on life toward which all of this had been moving me from the beginning, to come Beyond Tragedy.

And so it feels right to me that I bring this book to a close by attempting to share some fragments of the dramatic dialogue of this experience of living theater. First a letter from an old, old friend, a man who saved my life when I was a teen-ager by treating me with respect and inviting me into his home so that I could learn that being part of a family could be a warm and loving experience.

Dear Shelly,

I've read, and reread your piece "Teach Your Children Well." I was deeply troubled by it and rationalized that you were writing figuratively about relative life spans. That is what I want to believe.

I really don't know how to write this note. I've discarded several because none express what I'm trying to say.

Please don't feel you must respond. I just wanted you to know that we care and that our warmest and deepest wishes are with you always.

Lou[4]

I have another friend whom I have never seen. She is a poet, a therapist, a woman of the West Coast. After reading one of my books, she wrote me a touchingly vulnerable personal letter. Since then we reach out to each other by mail from time to time, exchanging feelings, thoughts and bits of our writings, fragments of our souls. In her letter of response to the piece about my not having long to live, she wrote:

Please tell me if there is anything in the world
I can do for you.

At the same time, she knew what she could do for me, and of
course she did it. She wrote and sent me this poem:

A Mourning
—for Sheldon Kopp

I knew you were dying. But I didn't
know you were dying *again*. I thought
that by having your head cut open once,
by letting the surgeons have a picnic
in your brain, by staring death darkly,
one to one in the eye, you had earned
escape, reprieve, at least another turn.

. . . .

Why did you choose me to tell? Did you
know, did you know, did the banners float
up in the sky advertising that I was the child
who stayed with my father until he was dead,
while the cancer ate him alive and he turned
yellow and violet and out of mind, from
the maddening pain, from the plain morphine?

He taught me dying. He taught me lying
in hospital beds and breathing from tubes
of oxygen. He taught me even then flowers,
the seasons of birds, the shadows of leaves
on the hospital lawn. He taught me how
life lies down at the end. He showed me
that death was a thing he could do.

. . . .

Like sleep, like pressing your knuckles into your eyes,
like night, like going blind, like sex the first time—
no guesses contain it. Images don't range out far enough.
Traps can't catch it alive and no matter what cage you
keep it in—bars, meshes, fences, walls or barbed
wires, it slips out and calls you and hauls you away.

. . . .

We ate dinner on the wharf.

    The dog outside my study barks.

We drove home on the ocean road
and the stars were bright.

    The barking dog barks at the moon.

The lights of our town reach on and on
and around the Rincon where they finally fall down.

    The dog stops barking.

. . . .

Don't, don't go yet!
I've only just met you.
I've only just told you my name.

. . . .

In those games that we play,
the ones where you say:
If you had just thirty days
to live, what would you do?
What did you used to say?
What do you say when it isn't
a game, when the hand on the
curtain gradually moves the
curtain across the stage?

What do you think of at night?
What do you think when you open
your eyes and you're not dead yet?
What do you love? Do you love,
by now, just life? And how does
it feel to think of leaving us all
behind? Do you rage? Do you weep?
Do you still say *why* — or is there
also that stranger called relief?

. . . .

Before you go
   let me tell you how glad I am you were born;
   let me tell you again what a gift you are;
   how less alone, how mended, how brothered,
      befriended I am in your also being alive;

   let me say how grateful I am that you
     blundered into your turn, that you dared,
    you confessed, you intended
   let me tell you again
Before it is time . . .

Before it is time,
     Now again shooting the anaesthetic into your veins

Before you have completely gone over to the other side,
   Now once again with saw opening the cranium

Before the angels lift you away,
   And seeing that there is nothing to be done this time

And you become one of them . . .[5]

And there was more, so much more. There is a man I feel close to. We know each other well. I have treated him, trained him, loved him. This then is what he wrote:

Dear Shelly,

"Teach Your Children Well" is one of the most beautiful
    things you've ever written.
And so it comes to this "What is it then between us?"
Respect, love, devotion, competition,
Trying, failing, succeeding.
Feeling, vastness, admiration and hatred. Bounty.
I came to you expectant, hopeful and you smashed me to the
    ground and dared me to get up and pushed me back and
    laughed at me on my knees and tormented me beyond any
    rights given to you.
And I came to learn the truth of hope and the futility of it.
You banished me to commitment and made it impossible for
    me to remain on my knees very long.
You cast me out, screaming wretching and vomiting with
    hatred and fear and stubborness and viciousness and
said the cold will temper your heat.
I would kill you if I wouldn't miss you so much
And now you say so plainly that you are dying. Eloquently,
    simply, you say, you do not even announce, that you
    are dying.
What is it then between us?
Living and dying
You were no sandman
You screamed in my ears and I awoke with fright and have
    scurried ever after. Up hill and down. Ever moving.
    You pointed and it was out there and I squinched my
    eyes and turned back.
Where is refuge, where can I rest, I want to rest. You
    haven't worked. Awake.
Oh the bloody awakeness. I can no longer sleep without
    wanting to wake.

You damned me and cursed me to living and seeking even
when I felt so small and insignificant and worthless.
You gave me a memory that tells me but only last Wednesday
things were cool—yes they were—I'll be there again
won't I—of course, unless I die, of course.
There is a cord between us that increases in length with the
days and years. Its vibrations, curiously do not lessen.
Their form is rounder. But the string is longer and as
the string grows slimmer and the waves rounder I float
and and spin alone and seek my level and wonder
less what is mine and what is yours and wonder more
whom am I and what am I about and where are my words,
where are my thoughts, where are my deeds.
I don't know man. It's all so fucking complicated. I'm
only a man; such sayings require a delicate touch,
they will not be possessed. They carry me only if I
ride, they will not tug me from my mooring.
You stuffed the keys to myself down my throat telling me
your keys weren't my keys and I trusted you. You trusted
yourself. Arrogant, shaking in your boots you trusted
yourself and invited me to do the same and trusted
only yourself unless I did the same.
You left me as you found me, alone—
You took the rocks out of my pack and put some bread in
their place. You shoved me firmly in my back. You did not
cuff me forward with a blow to the back of my neck.
You shoved dirt in my face without bloodying my nose and
said smell it, taste, it. And it was black and moist
and smelled rich and I said yes I've long known about
the earth and you screamed to dig on it for dig it
we must or we are lost and I yelled back to go fuck
yourself you fucking tyrant and you held my head
while I cried and stroked me and said there was no
help for it.
And so now what is there between us
Memories does not say it,
legacy does not say it

blessing no
curse no
Inspiration, experience, life together shared—all of it.
Some of it unknown to each or either of us. Some
of it to be spelled out, some secret and never to be
revealed, some unsayable, some unknown—
Breath
Breathing, pusling, movement and living, Death is not
living but dying is. And what the hell else is there
to say?

Love

Jack[6]

This time I responded to each of the people who had written to me. I wrote different things to each of them. I wrote the same things to all of them. Here is a composite of what I wrote:

Dear Friend,

Thank you for being with me once more. You are
generous and I will take all that I can get.

I regret that my last article caught you so off
guard. It is my wish to spare you any needless
suffering.

Because I have involved you so in my own
struggles, I want to keep things clear
between us, so that there is no more pain
than is required.

The "facts" are that in my second bout of
brain surgery in March of 1973, it was again
not possible to remove the entire tumor.
And so it will continue to grow. The need
for further surgery is inevitable.

I am highly unlikely to survive much more
of it. But I am determined to pay what
I must in pain and in terror to continue my
life as I can.

Yet I am no tragic figure. I do not live the life
of a dying man. My life has certainly been foreshortened, but it is not yet time for the final
curtain. Though I have less time left than I
would wish, I am *not* dying, I am living.

Love,

Shelly.

CHAPTER NOTES

Part I THE THEATER OF THERAPY

Chapter I *Miscasting*

1. I have deliberately omitted any discussion of psychodrama and traditional role-playing techniques in this book. The reader will find such matters described elsewhere in the literature comprehensively and in detail.
2. Phillip Roth. *Portnoy's Complaint*, Random House, New York, 1967.
3. Sheldon B. Kopp. *The Hanged Man: Psychotherapy and the Forces of Darkness*, Science and Behavior Books, Inc., Palo Alto, California, 1974.
4. George Orwell. *Nineteen Eighty Four*, New American Library, New York, 1964. Orwell projects a time when even facial expressions may be monitored for forbidden political dissidence.

Chapter II *Pretend You're Not Pretending*

1. Sheldon B. Kopp. *The Hanged Man: Psychotherapy and the Forces of Darkness*, Science and Behavior Books, Inc., Palo Alto, California, 1974.
2. Richard von Krafft-Ebing. *Psychopathia Sexualis: A Medico-Forensic Study*, Putnam, New York, 1969. The original edition which first inspired my present career is no longer in print. The Latin passages in the later edition are far less interesting than those in the original.
3. Sheldon B. Kopp, *Guru* (1971), *If You Meet the Buddha on the Road, Kill Him!* (1972), and *The Hanged Man* (1974), Science and Behavior Books, Inc., Palo Alto, California.
4. Gregory Bateson. *Steps to the Ecology of Mind*, Ballantine Books, New York, 1972, pp. 206-7.
5. Gregory Bateson, *Steps to the Ecology of Mind*, p. 217.
6. Gregory Bateson, *Steps to the Ecology of Mind*, p. 217.

Chapter III   *Irreverent Metatheater*

1. Lionel Abel. *Metatheatre: A New View of Dramatic Form*, A Drama-book, Hill and Wang, New York, 1963.
2. Walter Kaufmann. *Tragedy and Philosophy*, Doubleday & Co., Inc., Garden City, New York, 1969.
3. George Steiner. *The Death of Tragedy*, Alfred A. Knopf, New York, 1961.
4. Lionel Abel. *Metatheatre*.
5. George Steiner. *The Death of Tragedy*, pp. 352-353.
6. George Steiner. *The Death of Tragedy*, p. 241.
7. George Steiner. *The Death of Tragedy*, p. 243.
8. George Steiner. *The Death of Tragedy*, pp. 247-248.
9. Lionel Abel. *Metatheatre*. p. 47.

Chapter IV   *Therapy as Theater*

1. Originally reported by M.C. Stevenson in *The Zuni Indians*, 23rd Annual Report of the Bureau of American Ethnology, Washington, D.C.: Smithsonian Institution, 1905. Described by Claude Levi-Strauss in *Structural Anthropology*, Harper Torchbooks, Edition, Basic Books, Inc., New York, 1963, pp. 172-173.
2. Claude Levi-Strauss, *Structural Anthropology*, p. 174.
3. Sheldon B. Kopp, *Guru: Metaphors from a Psychotherapist*, Science and Behavior Books, Inc., Palo Alto, California, 1971.
4. Originally reported by Franz Boas in *The Religion of the Kwakiutl*, Columbia University Contributions to Anthropology, Vol. 10, New York, 1930, Part II, pp. 1-41. Described by Claude Levi-Strauss in *Structural Anthropology*, pp. 175-178.
5. Claude Levi-Strauss. *Structural Anthropology*, p. 180.
6. Mannheim. Quoted in an unpublished interview of Jules

Masserman by David Moss, III.

7. C. G. Jung. Quoted in *Success and Failure in Analysis:* The Proceedings of the Fifth International Congress for Analytical Psychology, Edited by Gerhard Adler, G. P. Putnam's Sons, New York, for the C. G. Jung Foundation for Analytical Psychology, 1974, p. 69.

8. In *Success and Failure in Analysis*, pp. 69ff.

9. Edgar A. Levenson. *The Fallacy of Understanding: An Inquiry into the Changing Structure of Psychoanalysis*, Basic Books, Inc., New York, 1972, p. 214.

10. Edgar A. Levenson. *The Fallacy of Understanding*, see particularly Chapter 12, "Clinical Elaborations: The Choreography of Psychotherapy,": pp. 167-180.

Part II   THE PLAY OPENS

Chapter I   *Theater Games*

1. Gregory Bateson. "A Theory of Play and Fantasy" in *Steps to an Ecology of Mind*, Ballantine Books, New York, 1972, pp. 177-193.

2. Gregory Bateson, page 180.

3. Edward Albee. *Who's Afraid of Virginia Woolf?*, Pocket Books, New York, 1964.

4. Eric Berne. *Games People Play: The Psychology of Human Relationships*, Grove Press, New York, 1964.

5. Thomas A. Harris, *I'm OK—You're OK*, Harper and Row, New York, 1969.

6. Claude Steiner. *Games Alcoholics Play: The Analysis of Life Scripts*, Ballantine Books, New York, 1971, p. 27.

7. Richard B. Sewall. *The Vision of Tragedy*, Yale University Press, New Haven and London, 1959, p. 6.

8. Eric Berne. *What Do You Say After You Say Hello?* Grove Press, New York, (A Bantam Book), 1972, p. 341.

9. Sheldon B. Kopp. *The Hanged Man: Psychotherapy and the Forces of Darkness*, Science and Behavior Books, Inc., Palo

Alto, California 1974, p. 48.

10. Carlos Castaneda develops this conception in detail throughout Don Juan series. *The Teachings of Don Juan: A Yaqui Way of Knowledge* (1969), *A Separate Reality: Further Conversations with Don Juan* (1971), *A Journey to Ixtlan* (1972), and *Tales of Power* (1974), Simon and Schuster, New York.
11. *The Hevajra Tantra*. Edited and translated by D. L. Snellgrove, Oxford University Press, 1969, Vol. I, p. 93. Quoted in Mystical Experience by Ben-Ami Scharfstein, Penguin Books, Inc., Baltimore, Maryland, 1974, pp. 23-24.
12. Jay Haley. *Strategies of Psychotherapy*, Grune & Stratton, Inc., New York, 1963.
13. Lanza del Vasto. *Return to the Source*, Translated by Jean Sidgwick, Pocket Books, New York, 1974 (Schocken Edition, 1972), p. 225.
14. Pearl King. "The Therapist-Patient Relationship," *The Journal of Analytical Psychology*, Vol. 18, No. 1, January 1973, pp. 1-2.

Chapter II *Taking Your Own Part*

1. Aleksander I. Solzhenitsyn.*The Gulag Archipelago*, Harper & Row, Publishers, Inc., New York, 1974, p. 162.
2. Solzhenitsyn. p. 173.
3. Eugene Ionesco. *Rhinoceros*, translated by Derek Prouse, Grove Press, Inc., New York, 1960.
4. Martin Esslin. *The Theater of the Absurd*, Anchor Books, Doubleday & Co., Inc., Garden City, New York, 1969, p. 353.
5. Ionesco. p. 98.
6. *Ibid.*, p. 102.
7. *Ibid.*, p. 103.
8. *Ibid.*, p. 104.
9. *Ibid.*, p. 105.
10. *Ibid.*, pp. 106-107.
11. *Ibid.*, p. 107.
12. Sheldon B. Kopp. "The Unceremonial Nature of Psychotherapy," *Journal of Contemporary Psychotherapy*, Vol. 5, No. 1,

Winter 1972, pp. 13-18.

13. Geroge Bernard Shaw. Quoted in *Facets of Comedy* by Walter Sorrell, Grosset & Dunlap, New York, 1972, p. 74.
14. Albert Camus. *The Myth of Sisyphus and Other Essays*, Translated from the French by Justin O'Brien, Vintage Books, New York, 1959, p. 3.
15. Sheldon B. Kopp, *If You Meet the Buddha on the Road, Kill Him: The Pilgrimage of Psychotherapy Patients*, Science and Behavior Books, Inc., Palo Alto, California, 1972, pp. 157-159.

Chapter III   *The Good Guys*

1. Martin Esslin. *Brecht: The Man and His Work*, New Revised Edition, Anchor Books, Doubleday & Company, Inc., Garden City, New York, 1971, p. xvi.
2. Robert Brustein. *The Theatre of Revolt* (An Atlantic Monthly Press Book), Little Brown & company, Boston, 1962, p. 263.
3. Bertolt Brecht. *The Threepenny Opera*, Grove Press, Inc., New York, 1960, p. 39.
4. O. Hobart Mowrer. *The New Group Therapy*, D. Van Nostrand Company, Inc., 1964.
5. St. Matthew 16, v. 19.
6. St. John 20, v. 23.
7. O. Hobart Mowrer. Pages 65ff.
8. St. Matthew, 6, v. 1-4.
9. O. Hobart Mowrer. Page 68.

Chapter IV   *And the Bad Guys*

1. Li Po. "Hard is the Journey" in *Li Po and Tu Fu*, Poems Selected and Translated with an Introduction and Notes by Arthur Cooper, Penguin Books, Baltimore, Maryland, 1974, p. 136.
2. Betinna L. Knapp. *Antonin Artaud: Man of Vision*, Discus Books, Published by Avon, New York, 1971, p. 11.
3. Peter Weiss. *The Persecution and Assassination of Jean-Paul Marat as Performed by the Inmates of the Asylum of Charenton under the Direction of the Marquis de Sade*, English version by Geoffrey Skelton, verse adaptation by Adrian Mitchell, Introduction by Peter Books, Atheneum, New York, 1965.
4. Peter Brook. *The Empty Space*, Discus Books, Published by Avon Books, New York, 1968, pp. 67-68.
5. Margaret Croyden. *Lunatics, Lovers & Poets: The Contemporary Experimental Theatre*, McGraw-Hill Book Co., New York, 1974, p. 240.
6. Peter Weiss. Act I, p. 31.
7. Simone de Beauvoir. Must We Burn Sade?" in *The Marquis de Sade, The 120 Days of Sodom and Other Writings*, Grove Press, Inc., New York, 1960, p. 42.
8. Simone de Beauvoir. Pages 3-64. (Originally published in the December 1951 and January 1952 issues of *Les Temps Modernes* as "Faut-il bruler Sade?";, translated into English by Annette Michelson.
9. Simone de Beauvoir. Page 64.
10. Sheldon Kopp. *The Hanged Man: Psychotherapy and the Forces of Darkness*. Science and Behavior Books, Inc., Palo Alto, California, 1974, p. 131.
11. Kris Kristofferson. *Shandy [The Perfect Disguise]*, Resaca Music Publishing Co., 1974. My italics.
12. Beth Joselow. "Gypsies," an unpublished poem.
13. James Joyce. *Ulysses*, The Modern Library, New York, 1934, p. 768.

Chapter V *Stepping In and Out of Character*

1. Milton Erickson. "Pantomime Techniques in Hypnosis and the Implications," in *Advanced Techniques of Hypnosis and Therapy: Selected papers of Milton Erickson, M.D.* Edited by Jay Haley. (New York: Grune & Stratton, 1967), pp. 93-94.
2. Jean-Paul Sartre. *Saint Genet: Actor and Martyr*, Translated from the French by Bernard Frechtman (New York: George Braziller, 1963), p. 6.
3. *Ibid.*, p. 17.   4. *Ibid.*, p. 41.
5. *Ibid.*, p. 611.
6. Jean Genet. *The Balcony*, translated by Bernard Frechtman, Revised Version (New York, Grove Press, Inc., 1966).
7. *Ibid.*, p. 7.   8. *Ibid.* p. 12.
9. *Ibid.* p. 10.   10. *Ibid.*, p. 96.
11. Sheldon B. Kopp. *The Hanged Man: Psychotherapy and the Forces of Darkness* (Palo Alto, California: Science and Behavior Books, Inc., 1974), pp. 111.
12. K.R. Eissler. "The Effect of the Structure of the Ego on Psychoanalytic Technique," *Journal of the American Psychoanalytic Association*, Volume I, Number 1, January 1953, pp. 104-143. The concept of "parameters of technique" was originally developed in a somewhat different form in the original psychoanalytic context.

Chapter VI *Playing to an Empty House*

1. Stephen Crane. *Stephen Crane: An Omnibus*, selected and edited with critical introduction and notes by Robert Wooster Stallman, Alfred A. Knopf, New York, 1966, p. 574.
2. Samuel Beckett. *Waiting for Godot:* A tragicomedy in two acts. New York: Grove Press, Inc., 1954.
3. *Ibid.*, p. 7.

4. *Ibid.*, p. 35.
5. *Ibid.*, p. 59.
6. *Ibid.*, p. 31.
7. *Ibid.*, p. 44.
8. *Casebook on Waiting for Godot.* Edited by Ruby Cohn. New York: Grove Press, Inc., 1967.
9. *Ibid.*, p. 166.
10. Martin Esslin. *The Theatre of the Absurd* (Revised updated edition). Garden City, N.Y.: Anchor Books, Doubleday & Company, Inc., 1969, pp. 1-3 for a more detailed account.
11. Karl Kraus. Quoted in Walter Sorell's *Facets of Comedy.* New York: Grosset & Dunlap, 1972, pp. 7-8.
12. Samuel Beckett. *All That Fall* in *Krapp's Last Tape and Other Dramatic Pieces.* New York: Grove Press, Inc., 1958, p. 83.
13. Becket. *Waiting for Godot,* p. 8.

Part III   TRAGEDY AND BEYOND

Chapter I   *The Tragic Hero*

1. Ruldolph Otto. *The Idea of the Holy: An Inquiry into the Non-rational Factor in the Idea of the Divine and Its Relation to the Rational,* Translated by John W. Harvey, Oxford University Press, London, 1950.
2. George Steiner. *The Death of Tragedy,* Alfred A. Knopf, New York, 1961.
3. Phyllis Hartnoll. *The Concise History of Theatre,* Harry N. Abrams, Inc., New York (Distributed by the New American Library, Inc., New York), An Abrams Art Paperback, no date.
4. Aritstotle. *Poetics,* Translated by S. H. Butcher, Introduction by Francis Fergusson, Hill and Wang, New York, 1961, p. 52.
5. Northrup Frye. *Anatomy of Criticism: Four Essays,* Princeton University Press, Princeton, N.J., 1971, p. 214.
6. H.D.F. Kitto. *Greek Tragedy,* Methuen and Co., Ltd., London, 1966, p. 122.
7. Henry Alonzo Meyers. *Tragedy: A View of Life,* Cornell Uni-

versity Press, Ithaca, N.Y., 1956, p. 139.
8. Sigmund Freud. The Psychotherapy of Hysteria," in *Studies in Hysteria*, Hogarth Press, London, Standard Edition, 1893, p. 305.
9. Aristotle. *Poetics*.
10. *Fredirich Nietzsche*. The Birth of Tragedy, *Translated by Clifton P. Fadiman, in* The Philosophy Nietzsche, The Modern Library, New York, no date, pp. 165-340.
11. Georg Hegel. *Philosoph of Right*, Oxford University Press, London, 1967.
12. Miguel de Unamuno. *The Tragic Sense of Life*, Dover Publications, London, 1954.
13. Sophocles, *Antigone*, Translated by E.F. Watling, in *The Theban Plays*, Penguin Books, 1971, pp. 126-162.
14. *Ibid.*, p. 127.
15. *Ibid.*, p. 128.
16. *Ibid.* p. 133.
17. *Ibid.*, p. 133.
18. *Ibid.*, p. 136.
19. *Ibid.*, p. 138.
20. *Ibid.*, p. 139.
21. *Ibid.*, p. 144.
22. *Ibid.*, p. 145.
23. *Ibid.*, p. 146.
24. *Ibid.*, p. 146.
25. *Ibid.*, p. 149.
26. *Ibid.*, p. 152.
27. *Ibid.*, p. 153.
28. *Ibid.*, p. 155.
29. *Ibid.*, p. 150.
30. *Ibid.*, p. 162.
31. Rollo May, *Love and Will*, W.W. Norton & Co., Inc., New York, 1969, p. 123.
32. C. G. Jung. *The Archetypes and the Collective Unconscious*, from the *Collected Works of C. G. Jung, Volume 9*, Part 1, Bollingen Series XX, Princeton University Press, Princeton, New Jersey, Second Edition, 1968.
33. Sheldon B. Kopp. *The Hanged Man: Psychotherapy and the Forces of Darkness*, Science and Behavior Books, Inc., Palo Alto, California, 1974.
34. Rix Weaver. *The Old Wise Woman: A Story of Active Imagination*, Published by G. P. Putnam's Sons for C. G. Jung Foundation for Analytical Psychology, New York, 1973, p. 31.

Chapter II *Freedom to Improvise*

1. Erasmus, *Desiderius.*
2. Arthur Sainer. *The Radical Theatre Notebook*, Discus Books, Published by Avon, New York, 1975, p. 62.
3. Walter Sorell. *Facets of Comedy*, Grosset & Dunlap, Inc., New York, 1973, p. 90.
4. Tom Wicker. *"One More Spring,"* an editorial. *The New York Times*, Friday, April 18, 1975, p. 31.
5. Michael Rossman. *"Music Lessons," American Review 18, The Magazine of New Writing*, edited by Theodore Solotaroff, Bantam Books, Inc., New York, September 1973, No. 18, p. 103.
6. Ibid., p. 110.
7. Ibid., pp. 106-107.
8. Sheldon B. Kopp. *Guru: Metaphors from a Psychotherapist*, Science and Behavior Books, Inc., Palo Alto, California, 1971, pp. 163-5.
9. Janwillem van de Wetering. *The Empty Mirror: Experiences in a Japanese Monastery*, Houghton Mifflin Company, 1974, p. 128.
10. Sonia Moore. *The Stanislavski System: The Professional Training of an Actor*, The Viking Press, New York, 1960, p. 65.
11. Ibid., p. 14.
12. Ibid., p. 15.

Chapter III *Before the Final Curtain*

1. (This note should be a page sequence reference to that section where it appears earlier in *This Side of Tragedy*.)
2. Sheldon B. Kopp. "Teach Your Children Well," *Pilgrimage: The Journal of Pastoral Psychotherapy*, Volume 3, Number 1, Fall 1974, pp. 11-12.
3. Sheldon B. Kopp. *The Hanged Man: Psychotherapy and the*

Forces of Darkness, Science and Behavior Books, Inc., Palo Alto, California, 1974.
4. Louis Cicchetti. Unpublished personal correspondence.
5. Daphne Rose Kingma "A Mourning—(for Sheldon Kopp)," an unpublished poem.
6. John Kehoe, M.D. Unpublished personal correspondence.

SUGGESTED READINGS

I. Theater and Therapy

Gregory Bateson, *Steps to the Ecology of Mind*, Ballantine Books, New York, 1972.
Claude Levi-Strauss. *Structural Anthropology*, Harper Torchbooks Edition, Basic Books, Inc., New York, 1963.
Edgar A. Levenson. *The Fallacy of Understanding: An Inquiry Into the Changing Structure of Psychoanalysis*, Basic Books, Inc., New York, 1972.

II. The Plays

Edward Albee. *Who's Afraid of Virginia Woolf?* Pocket Books, New York, 1964.
Samuel Beckett. *Waiting for Godot:* A Tragicomedy in Two Acts, Grove Press, Inc., New York, 1954.
Bertolt Brecht. *The Threepenny Opera*, Grove Press, Inc., New York, 1960.
Jean Genet. *The Balcony*, translated by Bernard Frechtman, revised version, Grove Press, Inc., New York, 1966.
Eugene Ionesco. *Rhinoceros*, translated by Derek Prouse, Grove Press, Inc., New York, 1960.
Sophocles. *Antigone*, translated by E. F. Watling in *The Theban Plays*, Penguin Books, Baltimore, Maryland, 1971.
Peter Weiss. *The Persecution and Assassination of Jean-Paul Marat as Performed by the Inmates of the Asylum of Charenton under the Direction of the Marquis de Sade*, English

version by Geoffrey Skelton, verse adaptation by Adrian Mitchell, introduction by Peter Brooks, Atheneum, New York, 1965.

III. *Tragedy and Beyond*

Lionel Abel. *Metatheatre: A New View of Dramatic Form*, a Drama-book, Hill and Wang, New York, 1963.

Martin Esslin. *The Theatre of the Absurd*, revised updated edition, Anchor Books, Doubleday and Company, Inc., Garden City, New York, 1969.

George Steiner. *The Death of Tragedy.*, Alfred A. Knopf, New York, 1961.